# Disney

# FROZEN

# THE OFFICIAL COOKBOOK

# Disney
# FROZEN
# THE OFFICIAL
# COOKBOOK

## A CULINARY JOURNEY
## THROUGH ARENDELLE

RECIPES BY DAYTONA DANIELSEN

WRITTEN BY S. T. BENDE

INSIGHT
EDITIONS

SAN RAFAEL · LOS ANGELES · LONDON

# CONTENTS

# INTRODUCTION

In 2013, the world met Elsa and Anna—the Arendellian sisters inspired by Hans Christian Andersson's classic fairytale *The Snow Queen*. The pair of princesses set off on a wintry adventure that showed the world the power of their sisterly bond and taught us all that an act of true love can thaw a frozen heart. After sparking countless sing-alongs—and a fantastical Frozen frenzy!—the film went on to win two Academy Awards before spawning a sequel (*Frozen 2*), three short films (*Frozen Fever*, *Olaf's Frozen Adventure*, and *Once Upon a Snowman*), a digital series of vignettes (*At Home with Olaf*), and a creative miniseries of reimaginings as told by everyone's favorite snowman (*Olaf Presents*). But despite being a work of fiction, the world of Frozen is actually rooted in fact. Although the kingdom of Arendelle is imaginary, its beautiful borders are inspired by the snowy fjord-side villages of Norway, and the foods mentioned in the films—from lutefisk to hot soup and nonalcoholic gløgg to giant cookies baked into the wavy shape of Norway—are inspired by real Scandinavian cuisine. With a rich cultural history, an intrinsic love of nature, and a society ingrained with the same adventurous spirit that led their Viking ancestors to explore the globe, the land that inspired Arendelle is one that's rife with magic. And it's only fitting that the recipes within these pages offer up sweet nods to the worlds—both fictional and true to life—that spark our imaginations. After all, some things are just so delightful, it's impossible to let them go.

Located on the water and flush with fjords and forests, the Scandinavian region has a rich natural history. The area's cuisine has been heavily influenced by both its seafaring culture and its citizens' commitment to spending time in nature. Seafood has long played a prominent role in regional menus—with Vikings cooking fish atop wooden planks (*plankefisk*), and cooks of the Middle Ages curing salmon by burying it beneath the sand. And current-day Norse cuisine adapts these practices to modern times. The breads, salads, and pastries of the region are often made with herbs and berries that have been hand-foraged on day hikes or camping trips, whereas *plankefisk* remains a popular cooking practice—with fillets now topped by a thoroughly modern cream sauce. For the first time in what feels like forever, *Frozen: The Official Cookbook* will allow everyone to bring these traditions into their very own homes . . . and to embark upon Frozen-inspired adventures of their own invention! 8,000 Salad Plates Salad (page 31) will bring together seasonal Scandinavian ingredients while honoring Anna's awe at the dinnerware she never knew she had. Not-Quite Lutefisk: Pan-Seared Cod with Cream Sauce and Blackberries (page 55) offers up a cheeky nod to a popular Norse delicacy. And "Act of True Love" Norwegian Heart Waffles (page 21) will allow home chefs from across the world to craft a distinctly Norwegian comfort food. With stews, cookies, and the quintessentially Scandinavian *kransekake*, this book serves up something for everyone—from adventurous princesses to cheerful snowmen to reindeer-loving fixer-uppers. Now grab an apron, forage up some ingredients, and let's go bring back summer!

CHAPTER ONE

# BREAKFAST

# CASTLE MORNINGS GRANOLA WITH RHUBARB COMPOTE

During the winter season, Arendellian mornings can be positively icy. Between long polar nights, chilly winter temperatures, and pre-dawn adventures playing with frozen magic, the first step out of bed is a frequently frosty experience . . . but one made easier by the promise of a hearty breakfast! Arendelle's playful princesses would be sure to get a burst of energy from this fun, fruity medley. This recipe crafts a homemade granola from oats, rye, nuts, and seeds, seasoned with the much-loved Scandinavian ingredient cardamom. Sprinkled over yogurt and a fresh rhubarb compote, Castle Mornings Granola is a great way to begin the day—and store up loads of energy to "do the magic!"

**GRANOLA:**
1½ cups rolled oats
¼ cup rye flakes
¼ cup pumpkin seeds
¼ cup sunflower seeds
2 tablespoons flaxseed
½ cup hazelnuts, coarsely chopped

2 tablespoons honey
1 teaspoon vanilla extract
1 teaspoon ground cinnamon
½ teaspoon freshly ground cardamom
½ teaspoon sea salt
½ cup dried sour cherries
¼ cup sesame seeds

**COMPOTE:**
5 medium stalks rhubarb, trimmed
⅓ cup sugar

Plain or vanilla yogurt, for serving
Honey, for serving (optional)

1. **TO MAKE THE GRANOLA:** Preheat the oven to 350°F. Line a large baking sheet (roughly 13 by 9 inches) with parchment paper.

2. In a medium heatproof mixing bowl, combine the oats, rye flakes, pumpkin seeds, sunflower seeds, and flaxseed and pour onto the baking sheet, spreading evenly, leaving some space on the side for the nuts. (Reserve the mixing bowl, as you'll need it soon.) Spread the hazelnuts evenly over the empty space. Bake for about 15 minutes, checking and scraping each component around occasionally. Remove the hazelnuts early if they start to darken. Watch regularly during the last 5 minutes to make sure the granola doesn't darken too much.

3. While the dry ingredients bake, put the honey in the reserved mixing bowl and stir in the vanilla, cinnamon, cardamom, and sea salt. Slide the bowl into the oven for the last minute. Turn off the oven, remove the bowl and baking sheet from the oven, carefully gather up the sides of the parchment paper, and use it to pour the oats, seeds, and nuts into the mixing bowl. Add the dried sour cherries and sesame seeds, then stir it all together with a large spoon until the dry ingredients are evenly coated with the spiced honey. Return the parchment paper to the baking sheet and spread the granola on

top. Return to the oven, which is still warm, and allow it to cool and dry completely.

4. Crumble and store in an airtight container for up to 2 weeks.

5. **TO MAKE THE COMPOTE:** Reheat the oven to 350°F. Cut the rhubarb stalks into 2-inch lengths and arrange in a baking dish that can roughly hold them in one layer. Sprinkle the sugar over top. Cover the dish with a sheet of aluminum foil and bake for 10 minutes. Peel back the foil and carefully turn over the rhubarb pieces. Replace the foil and bake for an additional 5 to 10 minutes, until the rhubarb is cooked through. Carefully lift the cooked rhubarb with a wide spatula or spoon and transfer to a serving dish. Let cool. The compote can be made up to 2 days in advance if you'd like.

6. To serve, spoon the yogurt into bowls, about 1 cup per serving. Top with the granola and compote. If you're using plain yogurt and want a little extra sweetness, drizzle a flavorful honey over it all.

NOTES: Feel free to swap out the rhubarb for whatever's in season.

This recipe is dairy-free if using dairy-free yogurt and gluten-free if using gluten free rolled oats.

# PICNIC RAISIN BUNS

As Coronation Day dawned, Anna raced through the castle and posed in front of a painted picnic. With nature playing such an important role in the Nordic culture—where families prioritize time spent outdoors, no matter the weather!—it makes sense that picnic menus are plentiful . . . and oftentimes packed with pastries. Inspired by one such recipe, these Picnic Raisin Buns would make for a tasty treat to share in the great outdoors. Seasoned with orange zest and a hearty dash of cardamom, these slightly sweet *boller* are delicious on their own or paired with *brunost*—a traditional Norwegian goat cheese that's named for its *brun* (brown) hue!

1 stick (8 tablespoons) butter
1¼ cups milk
2 teaspoons freshly ground cardamom
2 tablespoons active dry yeast
¾ cup sugar, divided

4½ cups flour, plus more as needed
½ teaspoon salt
Zest and juice of 1 large orange, divided
1 egg

¾ cup raisins
2 tablespoons melted butter, for brushing
Canola or vegetable oil, for greasing the bowl

1. In a small saucepan over medium heat, melt the butter. Add the milk and cardamom and heat until hot, then set aside to cool until lukewarm.

2. In a small bowl, mix the yeast, 1 tablespoon sugar, and ½ cup of the milk mixture. Let sit for about 5 minutes, until frothy.

3. In a large mixing bowl, combine the flour, remaining sugar, salt, and orange zest. Pour in the yeast mixture and the remaining milk and the egg and stir until a dough firms. (You might need to add a little more flour, until the dough is firm and releases from the sides of the bowl.) Turn the bowl onto a lightly floured surface and knead for 10 minutes, until smooth and elastic. Gather the dough and form it into a large ball.

4. Wipe out the bowl and lightly grease it with oil. Place the dough back inside, turning it until it's coated with oil. Cover with a clean, damp cloth and let it rise in a warm place free from drafts until doubled, about 1 hour.

5. While the dough rises, soak the raisins in freshly boiled water mixed with the orange juice. Drain before using.

6. Preheat the oven to 425°F and line two baking sheets with parchment paper.

7. Punch down the dough, mix in the drained raisins, and divide the dough into 12 portions. Place them on the prepared baking sheets, placing the smoothest side up. Cover with a damp towel and let rise again, about 20 minutes. Brush with the melted butter.

8. Bake, one sheet at a time, for about 10 minutes, until golden and they sound hollow when tapped on the underside. Cool on a wire rack and serve.

# RUSTIC WINTER RICE PORRIDGE

Anna's love for her sister knows no bounds. She'll willingly trek through miles of snow to reach the North Mountain, then boldly burst into a palace consisting entirely of ice. The cold might not bother Elsa, but after journeying through the elements, Anna would no doubt appreciate warming up to a cozy bowl of the Norwegian staple rice porridge (*risengrynsgrøt*). This rustic, cold-weather recipe combines arborio rice with a uniquely Scandinavian mixture of milk, almond extract, cinnamon, and freshly ground cardamom. Diners can even partake in a novel Norwegian tradition by tucking a single almond into the batch of porridge . . . and offering a prized marzipan pig to whomever discovers the treat!

¾ cup arborio rice

1½ cups water

½ teaspoon salt

3 cups whole milk, plus more as needed

¼ cup sugar, plus more as needed

1 teaspoon vanilla extract

½ teaspoon almond extract

½ teaspoon ground cinnamon

½ teaspoon freshly ground cardamom

**SERVING:**

1 whole blanched almond

2 tablespoons granulated sugar

2 teaspoons ground cinnamon

4 thin slices cold butter

1. In a medium pot, bring the rice, water, and salt to a boil over high heat. Lower the heat to medium low and simmer, uncovered, until the rice absorbs the water, about 10 minutes, stirring regularly to keep the rice from sticking.

2. Pour the milk into the rice and stir in the sugar, vanilla and almond extracts, cinnamon, and cardamom. Bring to a simmer and cover, stirring regularly, until the milk is absorbed and the rice is tender, about 30 minutes, checking occasionally and adding more milk if needed.

3. Taste, and add more sugar if you wish. Transfer the porridge to a serving dish or to four bowls, tucking the whole almond into one serving. Sprinkle with additional sugar and ground cinnamon and top with a pat of cold butter.

# EGGERØRE WITH PARSLEY, CHIVES, AND PEA VINES

From making magic around the castle to building a snowman who likes warm hugs, Anna and Elsa's days were filled with adventure. And as any proper princess—or reindeer-loving ice harvester!—knows, adventuring requires a *lot* of energy. These rich scrambled eggs would be sure to give anyone the boost they need to fuel their imaginations. Made with cream, butter, and pea shoots and frequently served alongside smoked salmon, the smooth and salty Eggerøre with Parsley, Chives, and Pea Vines is a protein-packed breakfast that's bound to bring about some truly enchanted play sessions. *Vær så god!*

**EGGS:**

6 eggs

6 tablespoons cream

¼ teaspoon salt

3 tablespoon chopped chives, divided

1 teaspoon butter

**PEA SHOOTS:**

1 tablespoon olive oil

¼ pound pea vines, thick stems discarded

Pinch salt

2 tablespoons chopped curly leaf parsley

Chive blossoms, for garnish (optional)

1. **TO MAKE THE EGGS:** In a medium mixing bowl, whisk the eggs, cream, and salt together until smooth. Add 1 tablespoon chives.

2. Melt the butter in a large pan over medium heat, tilting it so that the butter covers the bottom and comes slightly up the sides, just enough to keep the eggs from sticking.

3. Pour in the eggs. Using a wooden spoon, stir a little from time to time, lifting the eggs from the pan and tilting so that the top layer of eggs spills underneath and begins to cook. When the eggs are mostly set but still glistening, transfer to a plate and cover loosely with a sheet of aluminum foil to keep warm.

4. **TO MAKE THE PEA SHOOTS:** In a medium pan, heat the olive oil over medium heat until glistening. Add the pea vines and sauté briefly, until wilted. Season with a pinch of salt and remove from the heat.

5. To serve, divide the eggs between four plates. Top with the sautéed pea vines, parsley, remaining chives, and chive blossoms.

# "TWO SISTERS, ONE MIND" PANCAKES

When Anna and Elsa paired up for charades, Anna was positive theirs would be the winning team. After sharing childhood adventures, then reconnecting for the first time in forever, the two sisters were once again close enough to share one mind. This traditional Norwegian pancake recipe *(pannekaker)* pays tribute to Arendelle's daring duo by offering two topping twists on one delicious dish. The first invokes the flavors of fall with warm spiced apples, whereas the second serves up cool, summery blueberries. Rolled into logs and topped with a dollop of cream, "Two Sisters, One Mind" Pancakes are bound to be a winner at any kitchen table . . . or game night feast!

**PANCAKES:**

¾ cup all-purpose flour

¼ teaspoon kosher salt

1 to 2 tablespoons sugar

3 eggs

1½ cups whole milk

¾ teaspoon vanilla extract

¼ teaspoon almond extract

2 tablespoons unsalted butter, melted, plus more for greasing the pan

**BLUEBERRIES AND CREAM:**

¼ cup crème fraîche

½ teaspoon sugar

½ cup blueberry jam

Confectioners' sugar, for dusting

**SPICED APPLES:**

4 tablespoons butter

2 to 3 apples, peeled, cored, and thinly sliced

2 to 3 tablespoons brown sugar

½ teaspoon ground cinnamon

¼ teaspoon freshly ground cardamom

Whipped cream, for serving

Chopped almonds, for serving

1. **TO MAKE THE PANCAKES:** In a medium mixing bowl, whisk together the flour, salt, and sugar, then add the eggs, stirring briefly to break them up before pouring in the milk and the vanilla and almond extracts. Whisk until the batter is smooth and has no lumps. Stir in the butter. Refrigerate for 30 minutes.

2. Warm a well-seasoned cast-iron pan over medium heat, coating the bottom and sides. Pour in enough batter to thinly coat the bottom of the pan. (About ⅓ cup works well for a 10-inch pan.) Swirl the pan around until the batter coats the bottom. When the top begins to set and the edges begin to slightly color, about 2 minutes, gently slide a heat-safe silicone spatula underneath to loosen the pancake. Flip it and cook for about 1 minute, until the second side is done. Transfer to a plate.

3. Repeat with the remaining batter, adding a little butter to the pan as needed. Tent the cooked pancakes with a sheet of aluminum foil to keep warm.

4. **TO MAKE THE BLUEBERRIES AND CREAM:** In a small bowl, stir the crème fraîche and sugar together until smooth.

5. **TO MAKE THE SPICED APPLES:** In a skillet over medium heat, melt the butter. Add the apple slices and top with the sugar, cinnamon, and cardamom. Sauté for about 7 minutes, until the apples are soft and slightly caramelized.

6. With the blueberries and cream, fill pancakes with blueberry jam and roll up. Dust pancakes with confectioners' sugar and serve with a dollop of sweetened crème fraîche and chopped almonds.

7. With the spiced apples, fill pancakes with spiced apples and roll up. Serve with whipped cream and chopped almonds.

# "ACT OF TRUE LOVE" NORWEGIAN HEART WAFFLES

As Arendelle's resident love experts—the trolls—know, only an act of true love can thaw a frozen heart. And truly, one of the most loving things one can do is to bake this traditional Norwegian treat. Beloved the world over—from the fjords of Norway to the coast of California—Norwegian Heart Waffles will be the hit of any gathering. Made with butter, flour, and a hint of that Scandinavian staple, cardamom, these waffles are cooked in a heart-shaped waffle maker to give them their signature shape. Top them off with confectioners' sugar, whipped cream, chocolate-hazelnut spread, or a sweet, tart jam, and this beloved delicacy can be served at any time of day. It's sure to melt hearts all over the world!

1 stick (8 tablespoons) butter, at room temperature, plus more for greasing
1 cup sugar
4 eggs
1 cup nonfat plain Greek yogurt
½ cup milk
1 tablespoon orange zest

1 teaspoon almond extract
1½ cups all-purpose flour
½ cup almond flour
¾ teaspoon ground cardamom
½ teaspoon baking powder
½ teaspoon baking soda
Cooking spray, for greasing (optional)

**FOR SERVING:**

Confectioners' sugar
Whipped cream
Raspberry jam
Chocolate-hazelnut spread

**SPECIALTY TOOL:**

Heart-shaped waffle maker

1. In a large mixing bowl, ideally with a stand mixer, cream the butter and sugar until smooth and fluffy. Add the eggs, one at a time, mixing well after each addition. Stir in the yogurt, milk, orange zest, and almond extract.

2. In a separate bowl, whisk together the all-purpose flour, almond flour, cardamom, baking powder, and baking soda. Gradually add to the wet ingredients, mixing to incorporate.

3. Chill for 30 minutes.

4. Preheat a heart-shaped waffle maker and lightly grease it with butter or cooking spray. Cook the batter according to your model's instructions until golden.

5. Dust the waffles with confectioners' sugar and serve with a dollop of whipped cream and raspberry jam or chocolate-hazelnut spread.

CHAPTER TWO

# APPETIZERS, SIDES, AND SALADS

# FISH THROWERS GRAVLAX WITH SWEET MUSTARD SAUCE

Norway is revered around the world as the birthplace of skiing, the kingdom of the knitted sweaters, and, of course, the home of some of the best seafood around. Its fjords are home to fish that can grow so large, they require mountain-size fish throwers to toss them up to the docks. This mouthwatering appetizer tips its cap to the Arendellian fishmongers . . . and gets its name from its traditional means of preparation. While the Middle Ages saw salmon (*lax*) buried (*grav*) in the sand to ferment, contemporary gravlax is nestled in salt and sugar, seasoned with lemon and dill, and topped with a grainy mustard. A salty nod to a classic dish, Fish Throwers Gravlax with Sweet Mustard Sauce is proof that while cooking methods may evolve, some things never change.

1 fillet best-quality salmon, skin on, boneless, previously frozen (about 1 pound)

½ cup salt

½ cup sugar

1 bunch fresh dill, rinsed and roughly chopped

Zest of 1 lemon, finely grated

1 tablespoon dill pollen (optional)

Lemon wedges, for serving

**MUSTARD SAUCE:**

½ cup stone-ground mustard

2 tablespoons white vinegar

1 tablespoon sugar

2 tablespoons canola or vegetable oil

1 tablespoon finely chopped fresh dill

1. Place a sheet of plastic wrap large enough to wrap around the salmon in a shallow dish. Rinse the salmon and pat it dry. Place it on the plastic wrap.

2. In a small bowl, mix the salt, sugar, dill, lemon zest, and dill pollen (if using), then scatter it on top and underneath the salmon, evenly coating the entire surface area of the fish. Wrap the salmon in the plastic wrap. Refrigerate for at least 48 hours, turning it occasionally.

3. Unwrap the salmon and remove the excess curing ingredients and dill. Slice thinly and display on a platter with lemon wedges.

4. **TO MAKE THE MUSTARD SAUCE:** In a small mixing bowl, stir the mustard, vinegar, and sugar to combine. Pour in the oil, whisking to emulsify. Stir in the dill. Chill until ready to use and serve in a small bowl alongside the gravlax.

NOTE: Gravlax is cured rather than cooked, so be sure to use the best-quality fish and ensure that it's been previously frozen to kill potential parasites. Always use caution when eating food that hasn't been cooked, especially when pregnant or with health concerns.

# COOL AS A CUCUMBER SALAD WITH DILL

Olaf has always loved the idea of summer. While frolicking through fields of snow, the sunny snowman dreamed of all things hot. But given his chilly composition, he might need some help staying frozen in the warmer months. Cool as a Cucumber Salad with Dill is a refreshing dish that would be sure to keep Olaf's temperature from rising—no matter the weather. Thinly sliced English cucumbers are dressed with vinegar, salt, and sugar, then sprinkled with a popular Scandinavian seasoning. Crisp, crunchy, and endlessly invigorating, this offering will help just about anyone stave off the elements—even if they don't have much experience with heat.

2 English cucumbers
1 cup distilled white vinegar
½ cup water

2 teaspoons salt
2 teaspoons sugar

Small handful dill, coarsely chopped

1. Wash and scrub the cucumbers, then thinly slice.

2. In a small bowl, stir the vinegar, water, salt, and sugar.

3. Place the cucumber slices in a medium bowl and pour the vinegar mixture over the cucumbers. Stir so all the slices are coated. Chill for about 1 hour. Toss with the dill and serve.

# CORONATION DAY SHRIMP CANAPÉS

When a groggy Anna woke up on coronation day, she was immediately struck by the enormity of the pending event. The gates were open for the first time in forever, and the castle was done up for a party befitting a queen. Given Arendelle's proximity to the ocean, the lucky coronation guests would have likely dined on a feast of fresh seafood—including the classic Swedish appetizer *skagenrøre*! Inspired by the popular dish, Coronation Day Shrimp Canapés spread creamy shrimp salad atop lightly buttered toast to create a bite-size snack that could be eaten at any royal event—gloves on or off.

½ pound cooked shrimp (approx. 91 to 110)
1½ tablespoons mayonnaise
1½ tablespoons sour cream
1 teaspoon lemon juice
   teaspoon salt

2 tablespoons chopped fresh dill
2 tablespoons finely chopped red onion
3 scallions, thinly sliced, white and light green parts only

Triangles of buttered toast, or hors d'oeuvres crackers, for serving
Lemon wedges, for serving

1. Rinse and drain the shrimp. In a small mixing bowl, whisk together the mayonnaise, sour cream, lemon juice, and salt until smooth. Add the shrimp, dill, onion, and scallions and stir to combine.

2. To serve, spoon the shrimp onto triangles of buttered toast. Offer lemon wedges on the side.

> **NOTE:** This recipe is gluten-free if using gluten-free bread or crackers or cucumber slices instead.

# FIRE-ROASTED BREADSTICKS

When Elsa ventured into the unknown, she encountered the elemental spirits of the Enchanted Forest—the windy Gale, the Water Nokk, the enormous Earth Giants, and the fiery Bruni...who eagerly joined Elsa on her quest to seek out the secret siren. Fire-Roasted Breadsticks (*pinnebrød*) pay tribute to the little blue salamander's adventurous spirit—and its penchant for running *really* hot! Thick dough is kneaded with crushed juniper berries, wrapped around a stick, and cooked over a campfire. Warm, soft, and topped off with sea salt, these breadsticks are the perfect snack to share with friends, family, and talking snowmen. And, of course, Samantha.

2 cups all-purpose flour
1 tablespoon juniper berries, crushed
1 tablespoon sugar

2 teaspoons baking powder
¾ teaspoon salt
¼ cup canola oil

¾ cup milk
Cooking spray
Smoked sea salt

1. Before you start to cook, build a campfire and prepare eight sticks by stripping bark and sharpening one end of each. (Alternatively, use store-bought roasting sticks.)

2. In a large mixing bowl, stir the flour, crushed juniper berries, sugar, baking powder, and salt. Add the oil and milk to make a smooth dough. (Add more liquid if necessary, but the dough should not be sticky.)

3. Divide the dough into eight sections. Spray each stick with cooking spray, then twist the dough around each one in a spiral, tucking the ends to secure them. Sprinkle with smoked sea salt.

4. Bake over the embers, rotating occasionally, until lightly golden and cooked through, 10 to 15 minutes.

**VARIATION:** Enjoy the woodsy flavor without the campfire by twisting the dough around skewers and baking in a 375°F oven until cooked through, 12 to 15 minutes.

**NOTE:** This recipe is easily made vegan and dairy-free by swapping out the milk for water.

# 8,000 SALAD PLATES SALAD

When the castle gates were opened up for the first time in forever, Anna was shocked to discover the sheer volume of flatware, stemware, and, of course, salad plates her family has on hand. And with a coronation day feast to prepare, no doubt the chefs were busily cooking up crudités, fish platters, and *kransekake*...and coming up with a variety of vegetable-rich dishes to fill the thousands of plates making their way out of storage. With lettuce, sliced cauliflower, and fresh radishes, 8,000 Salad Plates Salad would make a fine coronation crowd-pleaser. And with hints of dill and a tangy vinaigrette dressing, this dish offers up an unexpected burst of flavor. Who knew?

**SALAD:**

1½ cups (4 to 5 ounces) cauliflower florets, thinly sliced

2 tablespoons extra-virgin olive oil

2 tablespoons lemon juice

4 cups leafy greens

6 to 9 radishes, thinly sliced

2 tablespoons chopped fresh dill

Toasted almonds, for serving

**VINAIGRETTE:**

3 tablespoons extra-virgin olive oil

2 tablespoons champagne wine vinegar or white vinegar

1 teaspoon Dijon mustard

¼ teaspoon salt

1. **TO MAKE THE SALAD:** Bring several inches of salted water to a boil in a large pan and prepare a bowl of ice water.

2. Blanch the cauliflower in the boiling water for about 1 minute and use a slotted spoon to transfer it to the ice water for 30 seconds. Drain and arrange the cauliflower in a single layer on a large plate. Drizzle the olive oil and lemon juice over top. Set aside.

3. In a large bowl, combine the leafy greens, sliced radishes, and dill.

4. **TO MAKE THE VINAIGRETTE:** In a small bowl, whisk together the olive oil, vinegar, Dijon mustard, and salt. Drizzle the dressing over the salad greens and gently toss to coat.

5. Arrange the salad on four plates and top each with the marinated cauliflower and toasted almonds.

# FOREVER WINTER BARLEY SALAD

Nordic seasons can feel a bit extreme. As summer shifts to winter, endless sun-filled days give way to icy polar nights . . . and Arendellian diets would shift from summery berries to wintry grains. Forever Winter Barley Salad incorporates the flavors that Scandinavians are likely to encounter during the colder months. Kale and pearl barley are paired with celery root, red cabbage, and sliced almonds to create a hearty, vitamin-packed meal that can be rustled up even in the midst of an eternal winter. After all, sometimes you *can't* just unfreeze it.

**SALAD:**

¾ cup pearl barley

2½ cups water

2 tablespoons extra-virgin olive oil

1 cup peeled and diced celery root (celeriac) (about ½ small celery root)

1 cup thinly sliced red cabbage (about ½ small red cabbage)

2 garlic cloves, crushed

2 cups chopped kale leaves

½ cup sliced almonds, toasted

½ cup unsweetened dried cranberries (see note)

3 ounces blue cheese, crumbled

**DRESSING:**

3 tablespoons roasted or regular walnut oil

2 tablespoons sherry vinegar or balsamic vinegar

1 tablespoon chopped fresh thyme

1 teaspoon kosher salt

1. **TO MAKE THE SALAD:** Rinse the pearl barley and place in a medium saucepan with the water. Bring to a boil over high heat, lower the heat to medium low, then cover and simmer until tender, 25 to 30 minutes. Drain any excess water, then cool the cooked grains to room temperature and transfer to a large bowl.

2. In a large pan, heat the olive oil over medium-high heat until it glistens. Add the diced celery root and sauté until tender, 5 to 7 minutes. Add the sliced cabbage and garlic and sauté for another 2 minutes, until slightly softened, then add the kale and allow to wilt for 1 minute, and set aside.

3. **TO MAKE THE DRESSING:** In a small bowl, combine the walnut oil, vinegar, thyme, and salt, whisking to emulsify. Pour the dressing over the barley and toss to combine. Add the celery root, cabbage, and kale, and gently toss to combine. Transfer to a platter and top with the sliced almonds, dried cranberries, and blue cheese. Serve at room temperature.

**NOTE:** Pomegranate seeds would also be lovely here instead of the cranberries.

# ARE REINDEERS BETTER THAN PEOPLE? GLAZED CARROTS WITH ORANGE AND PARSLEY

Raised by trolls and living the oft-solitary life of an ice harvester, Kristoff hadn't spent much time around humans. Not that he'd needed to—his best friend, Sven, regaled him with sympathetic stories and lively songs on their journeys across the frozen fjords. This recipe offers a tasty tribute to Kristoff's loyal companion by roasting Sven's favorite food—carrots—with a hint of honey and orange. With a crisp crunch and tangy taste, Are Reindeers Better Than People? Glazed Carrots are a sweet side that can be shared with friends or people you just met that day—no engagement necessary.

1¼ pounds carrots, peeled

2 tablespoons olive oil

2 tablespoons orange zest

2 tablespoons fresh orange juice (from the same orange)

2 tablespoons honey

1 teaspoon salt

½ teaspoon ground coriander

2 tablespoons sliced almonds, toasted

2 tablespoons chopped fresh parsley

Flake salt

1. Preheat the oven to 425°F. Slice the carrots in half lengthwise and place them on a baking sheet.

2. In a medium bowl, combine the olive oil, orange zest and juice, honey, salt, and coriander. Drizzle over the carrots and turn to coat. Arrange the carrots in a single layer.

3. Roast until tender and slightly caramelized, about 25 minutes, depending on the thickness of the carrots, turning midway.

4. Transfer to a serving dish. Scatter the almonds and parsley on top. Sprinkle with flake salt.

# "CERTAIN CERTAINTIES" BUTTER-BRAISED RED POTATOES

Scandinavian feasts are often accompanied by potatoes. Whether boiled, baked, or roasted over an open campfire, this side is a staple of any proper Scandi meal. Cooked with butter and salt and seasoned with red wine vinegar and fresh dill, these Butter-Braised Red Potatoes would have made the perfect addition to Elsa and Anna's Autumn Feast. After all, some things never change—from friendships to traditions to the presence of certain celebratory side dishes!

2 pounds small red new potatoes

4 tablespoons unsalted butter
¾ teaspoon salt
1 tablespoon red wine vinegar

Handful fresh dill, roughly chopped

1. Rinse and scrub off any dirt from the potatoes, then cut in half lengthwise.

2. In a large, wide pan with a lid, melt the butter over medium heat until it just begins to turn frothy. Add the potatoes and cook, stirring occasionally, for about 5 minutes, until they start to turn golden, and toss to coat. Pour in just enough water to create a shallow layer at the bottom of the pan. Add the salt. Turn up the heat to medium-high and bring to a simmer. Cover and reduce the heat as needed to maintain a simmer, for about 15 minutes, until tender but still firm.

3. Remove the lid and increase the heat to medium-high so that the water evaporates. Stir occasionally, basting the potatoes with the rich sauce.

4. Remove from the heat, toss with the vinegar, sprinkle the dill over the potatoes, toss gently, and transfer to a serving dish.

# PALACE STEPS POTATOES

The steps of Elsa's ice palace are a thing of beauty. Intricately crafted railings frame glittery, frozen stairs that ascend to a crystalline doorway. This iconic design is matched only by the impressively carved Hasselback potato—a Swedish dish with a striking resemblance to the entrance of a certain ice palace for one. Drawing on the spirit of that design, Palace Steps Potatoes layer butter, breadcrumbs, and Jarlsberg cheese between thinly carved grooves to create a dish that's rich, flavorful, and designed to be a delightful stepping stone to any feast.

4 large yellow potatoes
(7 to 8 ounces each)

3 tablespoons butter, melted

1 tablespoon chopped fresh
thyme leaves

1 teaspoon salt
Pepper

¼ cup grated Jarlsberg cheese
(see note)

3 tablespoons breadcrumbs

1. Preheat the oven 425°F. Line a sided baking dish with aluminum foil.

2. Rinse and scrub off any dirt from the potatoes. Pat dry and stabilize them on a cutting board between two wooden chopsticks. (This will help prevent cutting all the way through.) Cut into ⅛-inch slices, taking care to not cut all the way through. Place the potatoes on the prepared baking dish.

3. In a small bowl, mix the melted butter, thyme, salt, and pepper. Brush this mixture over the potatoes, making sure to brush in between each slice.

4. In another small bowl, mix the cheese and breadcrumbs and sprinkle over the potatoes—again, making sure to get the mixture between the slices.

5. Bake for about 45 minutes, until the potatoes are tender inside and the outside are crisp and golden.

NOTE: Gruyère would also work well in place of the Jarlsberg cheese.

# CHAPTER THREE

## SOUPS

# TOWN SQUARE SPINACH SOUP

Arendelle's popular town square is positively brimming with life and is the perfect place for citizens to procure almost anything they need, from fish to ice to a cold remedy of Wandering Oaken's own invention—when the cheerful trading post (and sauna!) proprietor is working from his booth in town, of course! Here, Arendellians would even be able to pick up the ingredients to make *spinatsuppe*—a traditional Scandinavian soup. Our version of this much-loved dish, Town Square Spinach Soup, brings together spinach, onion, and cream in a thick broth, which is topped off with hard-boiled eggs. It's a rich, hearty meal that's sure to bring the entire kingdom together . . . for a completely *unchaotic* hullabaloo.

Salt

1 pound fresh spinach leaves

2 tablespoons butter

1 onion, finely chopped

3 cups chicken broth

1 cup milk or heavy cream

2 tablespoons cornstarch

2 tablespoons water

Freshly ground white pepper

4 hard-boiled eggs, halved lengthwise

Chopped fresh herbs, such as parsley, for garnish

1. Bring a large pot of salted water to a boil over high heat. Add the spinach, using tongs to immerse it in the water, and cook until tender, about 2 minutes. In the meantime, prepare a bowl of ice water to shock the cooking spinach. Strain out the spinach and place in the ice water. Drain and allow to rest in a colander.

2. Wipe out and dry the pot. Place the butter inside and melt over medium heat. Add the onion and sauté until translucent, about 3 minutes. Add the broth and bring to a simmer. Pour in the milk or cream.

3. While the soup heats, squeeze out any excess water from the spinach and roughly chop. Add to a blender along with 1 cup of the soup, then purée until smooth. Working in batches, purée the remainder of the soup, returning the blended soup to the pot after each batch. (Take care when blending hot liquids, as they can spray out of the blender.) Return the soup to the pot.

4. To thicken the soup, make a slurry in a small bowl by stirring together cornstarch and water until smooth. Add to the soup and continue simmering another 3 minutes. Taste and season with salt and white pepper as desired.

5. To serve, ladle into bowls and top each with two halves of hard-boiled eggs. Garnish with fresh herbs.

> **NOTE:** This recipe is gluten-free if made with cornstarch that's manufactured in a gluten-free processing facility.

# PUMPKIN PATCH BEEF STEW

As Olaf enjoys his new permafrost inside a local pumpkin patch, he wishes the moment could last forever—and that he could eat this delicious dish. This savory stew would enable him to prolong his picnic-perfect memory . . . at least until it was gobbled up! Based on the traditional *lapskaus*—a beef-and-vegetable stew—this recipe places pieces of pumpkin alongside meat, potatoes, and carrots. Seasoned with bay leaf and topped with fresh parsley, Pumpkin Patch Beef Stew is bound to leave anyone feeling prone to poetic musings . . . especially in those moments when change mocks us with her beauty.

1½ pounds beef stew meat, cubed

Salt

Pepper

2 tablespoons butter

1 onion, finely chopped

4 carrots, peeled and cut into ¼-inch slices

1 pound waxy potatoes, such as Yukon Gold or new potatoes, peeled and cut into ½-inch pieces

2 cups diced pumpkin (about 1 medium 2-pound pumpkin), peeled, seeded, and cut into 1-inch pieces) (see note)

1 bay leaf

3 cups beef broth

Fresh parsley, chopped, for garnish

1. Season the beef with salt and pepper. In a large pot over medium-high heat, melt the butter and brown the meat on all sides. Remove the beef from the pot and set aside. Add the onion and sauté until translucent, about 3 minutes.

2. Return the beef to the pot. Add the carrots, potatoes, pumpkin, and bay leaf and pour the beef broth over the ingredients. Bring to a boil, then lower the heat to medium and bring to a simmer. Cook, covered, until the meat is tender and vegetables are tender, gently stirring occasionally, about 1½ hours. The pumpkin will break down during the cooking process, leaving a velvety texture and rich flavor.

3. Remove the bay leaf. Season with salt and pepper, and serve with chopped parsley for garnish.

NOTE: Substitute butternut squash in place of pumpkin, if desired.

# FROZEN FJORD FISH SOUP

When Elsa loses her glove—and control of her power!—she inadvertently freezes all of Arendelle . . . *and* the fjord surrounding the castle. Luckily in Norway, ice fishing is practically a national pastime—a necessity in a land where waterways spend a good portion of the year frozen solid! This flavorful take on a classic Nordic dish combines white fish, celery root, and carrots in a rich, creamy broth. Seasoned with bay leaf and topped with chopped dill, Frozen Fjord Fish Soup is sure to make a splash!

1 pound white fish fillets

4 cups fish broth or vegetable broth

1 celery root (celeriac), julienned

4 carrots, peeled and julienned

1 leek, halved lengthwise and thinly sliced

1 bay leaf

1 cup heavy cream

1 tablespoon white vinegar

Chopped fresh dill, for serving

1. Cut the fish into bite-size pieces and set aside.

2. Pour the broth in a large pot and bring to a simmer over medium-high heat. Add the celery root, carrots, leek, and bay leaf and simmer for 10 to 15 minutes, lowering the heat to medium low when it starts to boil, until the vegetables are tender yet still firm and not quite cooked. Add the cream and pieces of fish and cook until the fish is cooked through, 5 to 7 minutes. Carefully stir in the vinegar. Discard the bay leaf.

3. Ladle into bowls and garnish with dill.

# "HOT SOUP AND GLØGG IN THE GREAT HALL" YELLOW PEA SOUP

When Anna leaves Hans in charge of Arendelle, the thirteenth prince of the Southern Isles assures the kingdom's worried citizens that the castle will remain open to offer soup and hot gløgg in the Great Hall. Inspired by his offerings, this steamy vegetable soup would be sure to warm even the frostiest Arendellian. With split peas, leeks, and diced pancetta, Yellow Pea Soup invokes the flavors of Norway. And it just so happens to pair well with nonalcoholic hot gløgg!

2 cups yellow split peas

4 ounces diced pancetta

1 yellow onion, finely chopped

1 leek, cut in half lengthwise and thinly sliced

6 cups chicken broth

2 cups peeled and diced waxy potatoes, such as Yukon gold or new potatoes (about 4 potatoes)

1½ cups peeled and diced turnip (about 1 turnip)

4 carrots, peeled and diced

1 bay leaf

Few sprigs thyme

2 teaspoons salt, plus more as needed

Pepper

Sour cream, for serving

1. Rinse the peas in cold water and drain.

2. In a large soup pot over medium-high heat, fry the pancetta until the fat begins to render and the meat starts to turn golden. Add the onion and sauté until translucent, about 3 minutes, then add the leek and sauté another 2 minutes. Add the drained yellow peas and broth. Bring to a boil, then lower the heat to medium-low to simmer, partially covered, for 20 minutes.

3. Add the potatoes, turnip, carrots, bay leaf, and thyme. Cook for 45 to 60 minutes more, covered and stirring occasionally, until the peas are mushy and the vegetables are tender.

4. Remove and discard the bay leaf and thyme sprigs. Season with salt and pepper to taste. Serve in bowls and garnish with sour cream.

# CHAPTER FOUR

# ENTRÉES

# "WITHIN THESE WALLS" PYTT I PANNE

Elsa cherishes her home—and absolutely adores the people (and her favorite snowman and reindeer!) who live there with her. A cozy night within the castle walls might include a rousing game of charades or a spirited serenade with Kristoff and Sven. But whatever the activity, a night at home is always made better by a good meal. *Pytt i Panne*—a popular Scandinavian hash—would make an excellent accompaniment to a fun-filled family night. Diced meat and potatoes are seasoned with onions, Worcestershire sauce, and thyme, then served alongside fried eggs and pickled beets. Rich, salty, and filling, this nostalgic meal is sure to fuel an epic game night . . . or enthusiastic family sing-along!

4 tablespoons butter

2 cups diced starchy potatoes, such as russet (about 2, depending on the size)

2 yellow onions, chopped

1 pound leftover cooked meat (such as steak, pork, or sausages), diced

1 tablespoon fresh thyme leaves

Salt

White pepper

Worcestershire sauce, to taste (optional)

Fried eggs, for serving

Pickled beets, for serving (optional)

Whole-grain mustard, for serving (optional)

1. In a large frying pan, melt the butter over medium heat. Add the diced potatoes and cook for about 10 minutes, stirring occasionally, until golden and crispy. Add the onions and sauté until translucent and starting to caramelize. Add the meat and thyme and cook until heated through. Season with salt, pepper, and Worcestershire sauce (if using) to taste.

2. Serve with fried eggs on top and pickled beets and mustard on the side, if you'd like.

> **NOTE:** Feel free to swap the meat for plant-based proteins, such as tofu or tempeh, for a vegetarian variation.

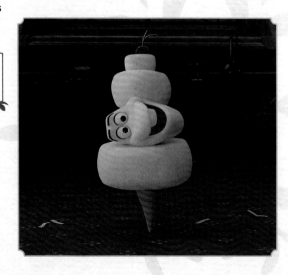

# "EVERY AUTUMN BREEZE" FÅRIKÅL

*Fårikål*—Norway's national dish—is revered throughout the country. This popular meal of lamb and cabbage even has its own feast day, with *Fårikålens Festdag* falling on the fourth Thursday of every September. Drawing on ingredients native to Norway, from the sheep who roam the mountains to the cabbage that's been grown since the Viking age, *fårikål* is an integral part of Norse society . . . and this cozy recipe will bring Norway's famous stew into any home! Lamb and cabbage are boiled into a savory stew, where they're seasoned with salt, peppercorns, and parsley. Best served alongside some thoroughly Norwegian boiled potatoes, "Every Autumn Breeze Fårikål" is a comforting meal for those days when the wind blows just a bit colder.

3 pounds lamb (shoulder, shank, or neck)

¼ cup flour

2 teaspoons salt

1 large green cabbage (about 3 pounds)

4 tablespoons butter

3 teaspoons whole black peppercorns

Chopped fresh parsley, for garnish

1. Cut the lamb into 1½-inch pieces and place in a large bowl. Dust the flour and salt over the lamb, tossing so that all sides are coated. Cut the cabbage into 1-inch wedges, removing and discarding the tough core.

2. In a large pot over medium-high heat, melt the butter. Add the lamb, working in batches, and brown all sides. When all the lamb is browned, return it to the pot, layering it with the cabbage and sprinkling the peppercorns throughout. Pour in enough water to just barely cover the lamb and cabbage (about 8 cups). Bring to a boil over high heat, then lower the heat to medium-low and bring to a gentle simmer. Cover and cook for about 2 hours, stirring occasionally, or until the lamb is tender and pulls away easily from the bones.

3. To serve, carefully lift the lamb pieces and cabbage out of the pot and arrange them in four bowls. Pour some of the flavorful broth and add some peppercorns to each bowl. Garnish with chopped fresh parsley.

# FIRE-ROASTED SALMON WITH CREAMY HERB SAUCE

The little salamander Bruni is known for its fiery personality. With a penchant for bursting into brilliant blue flames, the Fire Spirit is known for running hot—a trait that balances out its icy friend, Elsa. Drawing on the traditional Viking cooking method of *plankefisk*, Fire-Roasted Salmon with Creamy Herb Sauce pays tribute to Bruni's spirited nature. Lightly seasoned salmon is attached to a wooden board, then cooked over an outdoor fire. Sprinkled with lemon and served alongside an herb cream, this dish is sure to be the hit of any backyard barbecue . . . or Enchanted Forest feast.

**FISH:**

1½ pounds salmon fillet
Salt
Freshly ground black pepper
Olive oil
Lemon slices, for serving

**CREAM SAUCE:**

¼ cup sour cream
¼ cup mayonnaise
2 teaspoons mustard
¼ teaspoon salt
2 teaspoons lemon juice

1 tablespoon chopped fresh dill
1 tablespoon freshly grated horseradish (optional)

**SPECIALTY TOOL:**

Cooking twine

1. **TO MAKE THE FISH:** Prepare a fire outdoors. Meanwhile, prepare a wooden grilling plank that's at least 4 inches longer than the salmon fillet by soaking it in water for at least 30 minutes. (Alternatively, use two boards and cut the salmon in half).

2. When the fire reaches a steady, medium heat, season the salmon with salt and pepper.

3. Brush the plank with a thin layer of olive oil. Lay the salmon fillet skin side down in the middle of the board, leaving equal space at the top and bottom. Secure the fish to the board with cooking twine.

4. Set the board vertically at the edge of the fire, not directly in contact, supporting it with heavy rocks. The fish should face the flames.

5. Cook the fish, rotating the plank midway, for 20 to 40 minutes, depending on the heat of the fire, until the salmon is opaque and flakes easily.

6. **TO MAKE THE CREAM SAUCE:** Stir the sour cream, mayonnaise, mustard, salt, lemon juice, dill, and horseradish (if using) together in a medium bowl. Cover and refrigerate until ready to serve.

7. Remove the fish from the plank and serve with lemon slices and the creamy herb sauce.

**VARIATION:** If a fire isn't feasible, bake the salmon: Preheat the oven to 400°F. Lightly brush a baking pan with olive oil and place the salmon on top. Brush more oil on the salmon, then season with salt and pepper. Bake until cooked through, about 20 minutes, depending on the thickness of the salmon.

# NOT-QUITE LUTEFISK: PAN-SEARED COD WITH CREAM SAUCE AND BLACKBERRIES

After tossing a frosty Kristoff out of his Trading Post (and Sauna!), Wandering Oaken offers Anna an apology for the violence . . . and throws in a quart of *lutefisk* with her order so the two can "have good feelings." The quintessentially Norwegian, lye-soaked codfish is traditionally served at *julebord*—the Scandinavian Christmas feasts. Not-Quite Lutefisk puts a modern twist on the Scandi classic, turning this seasonal dish into one that can be served at any time. Here, seasoned cod is seared on a hot skillet, then topped with cream sauce and served alongside a fresh berry-and-vegetable salad. The inspired mix of old world meets *ny* (new) is so delightful, it's sure to inspire a heartfelt *hoo-hoo*!

**CREAM SAUCE:**

⅓ cup mayonnaise

⅔ cup sour cream

½ teaspoon Dijon mustard

1 tablespoon lemon juice

½ tablespoon chopped fresh dill

Salt

White pepper

**SALAD:**

12 blackberries

½ cucumber, peeled, halved lengthwise, and thinly sliced

½ fennel bulb, thinly sliced

6 radishes, thinly sliced

2 green onions, thinly sliced

Small handful fresh herbs (dill, mint, and parsley), chopped

2 tablespoons extra-virgin olive oil

Flake salt

**FISH:**

4 cod fillets, 6 ounces each

Salt

Pepper

2 tablespoons olive oil or butter

1. **TO MAKE THE CREAM SAUCE:** In a small bowl, mix the mayonnaise, sour cream, mustard, lemon juice, dill, salt, and pepper together until combined. Chill until ready to use.

2. **TO MAKE THE SALAD:** In a small bowl, combine the blackberries, cucumber, fennel, radishes, green onions, herbs, and olive oil. Sprinkle with flake salt to taste. Chill until ready to use.

3. **TO MAKE THE FISH:** Rinse and pat the cod dry. Season both sides with salt and black pepper.

4. Heat the oil or butter in a large skillet over medium-high heat until it begins to sizzle. Place the cod skin side down in the pan and sear for 3 to 4 minutes. Using a spatula, carefully flip and cook the other side until cooked through and flakes easily with a fork, about 4 minutes.

5. To serve, transfer the cod to plates and serve with the cream sauce and salad.

# SCANDINAVIAN FISH CAKES WITH MUSTARD CREAM SAUCE

Living alongside a fjord, the citizens of Arendelle would surely have access to the freshest catches of fish . . . and a vast variety of offerings. But there's little doubt that Arendellian tables would be frequently filled with fish cakes—a mashed offering of cod, onions, eggs, and cream, which are battered and baked into the ever-popular patties. Topped with a tangy mustard cream sauce and served alongside potatoes and fresh vegetables, Scandinavian Fish Cakes are a uniquely Norse dish that pays tribute to the traditional means of preparing small fish.

**FISH CAKES:**

1½ pounds cod fillets, cut into small pieces

1 small white onion, finely chopped

¼ cup heavy cream

¼ cup finely chopped fresh dill

2 tablespoons freshly squeezed lemon juice

2 teaspoons salt

2 large eggs

4 to 6 tablespoons all-purpose flour

Cooking spray

**MUSTARD CREAM SAUCE:**

½ cup sour cream

¼ cup mayonnaise

¼ cup whole-grain mustard

1 teaspoon honey

1 tablespoon lemon juice

Salt

1. **TO MAKE THE FISH CAKES:** Place the fish in a food processor and pulse until the fish is a coarse paste. Add the onion, cream, dill, lemon juice, salt, and eggs and process again to combine. Add 4 tablespoons flour and pulse again to combine; if it's too wet, add the remaining 2 tablespoons flour. Shape the fish into 12 patties and arrange on a baking sheet or plates to refrigerate for 30 minutes.

2. **TO MAKE THE MUSTARD CREAM SAUCE:** In a medium bowl, stir together the sour cream, mayonnaise, mustard, honey, lemon juice, and salt. Cover and refrigerate until ready to serve.

3. Preheat the oven to 400°F. Line a large baking sheet with aluminum foil and spray with the cooking spray. Carefully place the patties on the baking sheet and bake for 25 to 30 minutes until golden and cooked through. Serve with the mustard sauce.

# FOREIGN LANDS BACALAO

Elsa's coronation brings a variety of guests to the castle—from a prince of the Southern Isles to dignitaries from across the world. After all, Arendelle has a long history of exploring and trading with faraway lands, and it's only fitting to invite their representatives to the crowning of the new queen. Foreign Lands Bacalao honors Norway's rich tradition of seafaring trade. A generous portion of salt cod is simmered alongside onions, garlic, potatoes, and peppers, then seasoned with a myriad of spices. Served with bread and sprinkled with salt, this dish could be shared with trade partners far and wide—from sunny Spain to weaselly Weselton.

1 pound bacalao (salt cod)
¼ cup extra-virgin olive oil
2 large yellow onions, sliced
4 garlic cloves, thinly sliced
2 large waxy or all-purpose potatoes, such as Yukon Gold or new potatoes, peeled and diced

1 red bell pepper, sliced
One 14-ounce can diced tomatoes
1 bay leaf
1 teaspoon dried oregano
½ teaspoon smoked paprika
Salt

Pepper
¼ cup chopped fresh parsley
Red pepper flakes (optional)
Crusty bread, for serving

1. Rinse the salt cod under cold running water to remove the salt. Place in a bowl of fresh cold water, cover, and place in the refrigerator to soak for 24 to 48 hours, changing the water at least twice.

2. Cut the salt cod into 2-inch pieces.

3. In a large pot or Dutch oven over medium heat, heat the oil. Add the onions and cook until translucent, about 4 minutes. Add the sliced garlic and continue to cook for 30 seconds, until fragrant.

4. Add the potatoes and bell pepper and sauté for about 5 minutes, until softened. Add the tomatoes, bay leaf, dried oregano, smoked paprika, salt, and pepper.

5. Adjust the heat if needed to maintain a simmer for about 20 minutes, shaking the pot occasionally, until the potatoes are tender. Add the fish and continue to cook for about 15 minutes, or until cooked through and flakes easily.

6. Remove the bay leaf. Add the parsley and stir gently. Divide among four serving bowls. Offer red pepper flakes for serving. Serve with crusty bread for sopping up the juices and sea salt for seasoning to taste.

NOTE: Leftovers are excellent when reheated the next day.

# COZY FRICASSEE OF CHICKEN

As the breeze blows cold through the frosty fjords, *hønsefrikassee*—a popular comfort food—is served in homes throughout the Northern countries. This version of the tried-and-true Scandinavian dish flavors seasoned chicken with butter, onions, and garlic. Nestled alongside an array of vegetables and simmered in a creamy broth, this steamy, protein-packed feast is sure to make princesses, ice harvesters, and snowmen all sing with delight. With tender meat and savory flavors, Cozy Fricassee of Chicken is the culinary equivalent of a warm hug.

1 whole chicken (4 to 5 pounds), cut into pieces (see note)
Salt
Freshly ground pepper
4 tablespoons butter
1 large yellow onion, cut into wedges

1 leek, white and light green parts only, thinly sliced
1 rutabaga, peeled and cut into ¾-inch dice
3 carrots, cut into ½-inch slices
2 cloves garlic, minced
⅓ cup flour
3 cups chicken broth

1 bay leaf
¾ cup cream
Chopped fresh parsley, for serving
Boiled potatoes, for serving (optional)

**SPECIALTY TOOL:**

Kitchen thermometer

1. Season the chicken with salt and pepper.

2. In a large pot or Dutch oven over medium heat, melt the butter. Working in batches to avoid overcrowding, add the chicken pieces and brown all over, 2 to 3 minutes per side. Remove and set aside. Add the onion, leek, rutabaga, carrots, and garlic and sauté for about 7 minutes, until they begin to soften. (You may find that tongs work best here.) Sprinkle the flour over the vegetables and stir constantly, again using tongs, for about 4 minutes, to evenly distribute the flour and begin cooking it. Gradually pour in the chicken broth while stirring. Return the chicken pieces to the pot, along with the bay leaf, and nestle them in with the vegetables so they're mostly covered. When the broth comes to a simmer, cover and cook for 10 minutes.

Uncover and cook until the chicken is cooked through and reaches an internal temperature of 165°F, about 20 minutes. Remove the chicken and pour in the cream. Stir and bring it back to a simmer, stirring occasionally, for 3 more minutes. (Take care that it doesn't boil.) Taste and add salt and pepper as needed. Remove and discard the bay leaf. Return the chicken to the pot.

3. When you're ready to serve the chicken, divide it among four shallow bowls and ladle plenty of the vegetables and creamy sauce over each. Garnish with parsley.

NOTE: If you can find 4 pounds of bone-in, skin-on breasts, thighs, wings, and drumsticks, this will make quick work for you.

# "SOUP, ROAST, AND ICE CREAM" ROAST CHICKEN WITH BROWN GRAVY AND HERB SAUCE

There's a lot that goes into planning a wedding—even when one is marrying someone they've just met that day. But if there's one thing Anna knew for certain when planning her ill-fated wedding to Hans, it was that she wanted to serve up all of her favorite dishes, including soup, roast, and ice cream! In a flavor-packed nod to Anna's would-be matrimonial menu, this savory roasted chicken is rubbed with parsley butter and served alongside two delightful sauces. It's a classic dish that's guaranteed to please any crowd—wedding, coronation, or otherwise!

**CHICKEN:**

One 3- to 4-pound whole chicken

1 tablespoon olive oil

2 tablespoons salt

**PARSLEY BUTTER:**

½ stick butter, at room temperature

½ cup finely chopped fresh parsley

2 teaspoons salt

**CREAM SAUCE:**

¼ cup butter

¼ cup all-purpose flour

2 cups chicken broth

4 ounces *geitost* or *brunost*, shredded (see note)

1 tablespoon fresh thyme leaves

¾ teaspoon salt

¼ teaspoon ground white pepper

**HERB SAUCE:**

1 cup packed fresh herbs (thyme, dill, parsley)

¼ cup olive oil

½ teaspoon salt

**SPECIALTY TOOLS:**

Kitchen shears or sharp knife

Kitchen thermometer

1. **TO MAKE THE CHICKEN:** Begin by spatchcocking the chicken. Place the chicken on a cutting board with the breast side down and the neck facing you. Use the shears to cut along one side of the backbone and then the other, then remove it. Turn the chicken breast side up and press down to flatten the chicken and break the breastbone. Pat the chicken dry. Brush with olive oil and sprinkle with salt, then slide into the refrigerator, uncovered, for 2 to 3 hours.

2. About 30 minutes before roasting, remove the chicken from the refrigerator to allow it to begin to come to room temperature. Preheat the oven to 400°F.

3. **TO MAKE THE PARSLEY BUTTER:** In a small bowl, mash the butter with the chopped parsley and salt. Gently separate the skin of the chicken from the breast and thighs using your hands, then rub most of the butter inside. Spread the remaining butter over the skin.

4. Place the chicken on a broiler or roasting pan with a stovetop-safe base and roast until the internal temperature reaches 165°F, 45 to 60 minutes. Remove from the oven and let rest, covered, on a platter or wooden cutting board for about 15 minutes.

5. **TO MAKE THE CREAM SAUCE:** In a medium saucepan, melt the butter over medium heat. Whisk in the flour. Add the chicken broth, about ¼ cup at a time, whisking constantly, waiting for it to thicken before adding more. Finally, add the *geitost* and thyme and stir until the *geitost* melts. Season with the salt and white pepper.

6. **TO MAKE THE HERB SAUCE:** Place the herbs into a food processor with the olive oil and salt and whirl until the herbs are broken down into little flakes.

7. Carve the chicken and serve with the sauces on the side.

8. Serve with boiled potatoes garnished with dill, or the "Certain Certainties" Butter-Braised Red Potatoes (page 37).

> **NOTE:** *Geitost* or *brunost* is Norwegian brown cheese, made with goat milk or a mix of cow and goat milks.

# "WE FINISH EACH OTHER'S SANDWICHES" CHICKEN SALAD ON RYE BREAD

Anna has long hoped to meet someone with whom she can share her thoughts, her dreams, and her beloved sandwiches. Unfortunately, she learned the hard way that you can't marry a man you just met . . . and her relationship with Hans came to an icy end. But when Anna finally realized her feelings for Kristoff, she would no doubt have been excited to share *smørbrød*—a Scandinavian open-faced sandwich. "We Finish Each Other's Sandwiches" Chicken Salad on Rye Bread blends chopped chicken with curry powder and Worcestershire sauce, mixes in mayonnaise, and nestles the savory delicacy atop a bed of luscious lettuce. It's a popular picnic dish that's perfect to share with someone you love . . . just *not* the thirteenth prince of the Southern Isles!

1 pound cooked chicken
⅔ cup mayonnaise
⅓ cup sour cream
1 tablespoon lemon juice
1 teaspoon curry powder
½ teaspoon Worcestershire sauce

2 celery stalks, finely chopped
½ cup sliced cooked button or cremini mushrooms
1 cup green peas
¼ cup chopped fresh herbs (parsley and tarragon)
Salt
White pepper

4 tablespoons butter, at room temperature
4 slices rye bread
4 lettuce leaves
Lemon slices, for garnish
Fresh parsley leaves, for garnish

1. Dice or shred the chicken.

2. In a medium bowl, mix the mayonnaise, sour cream, lemon juice, curry powder, and Worcestershire sauce. Stir in the chicken, celery, mushrooms, peas, and herbs, and add salt and white pepper to taste.

3. To make the sandwiches, spread 1 tablespoon butter onto each slice of bread. Top with a lettuce leaf and spoon about 1 cup chicken salad on each. Garnish with lemon slices and parsley leaves.

# TRADING POST HAM AND POTATO DUMPLINGS

Wandering Oaken is the proprietor of a trading post (and sauna) located between Arendelle and the North Mountain. His log cabin offers visitors a cheerful place to buy carrots, clothing, and climbing supplies. When Elsa's icy outburst coats the entire region in frost, Oaken holds a Big Summer Blowout—with half-off deals on swimming suits, clogs, and a sun balm of Oaken's own invention! Trading Post Ham and Potato Dumplings offer a cheerful nod to the Arendellian's charming shop. Ground potatoes are mixed with flour, baking powder, and salt, then served alongside pork roast and lingonberry preserves. This delightful Nordic dish is soft, salty, and sure to hit the spot in *any* season. Hoo-hoo!

1 medium piece (about 6 ounces) salted pork or lamb

1 teaspoon salt, plus more for salting the meat

4 cups ground raw potatoes (about 4 medium-size potatoes; see note)

¾ cup all-purpose flour, plus more as needed

¾ cup graham whole-wheat flour

1 teaspoon baking powder

Salted butter, at room temperature, for serving

Lingonberry preserves, for serving

1. Place the salted meat in a large pot of water, bring to a boil over high heat, and reduce the heat to a simmer over medium-low, cooking until tender.

2. **IN THE MEANTIME, MAKE THE DUMPLINGS:** In a mixing bowl, combine the ground potatoes with the all-purpose flour, graham flour, baking powder, and salt, adding more all-purpose flour if needed to make a mixture that is firm yet moldable.

3. When the meat is cooked through, remove from the water and set aside. Form the dough into 12 to 16 balls, each about 2 inches in diameter. Carefully add these to the water and cook until they float to the surface, 30 to 45 minutes. Drain the dumplings.

4. Cut the meat into bite-size pieces.

5. Serve the dumplings with the meat, butter, and lingonberry preserves.

> **NOTE:** To prepare the potatoes, peel them and shred in a food processor, then run through with the blade until they're ground.

# BURNING LOVE

Arendelle's ice harvesters spend bleakly brisk mornings—and glacial Nordic nights—carving frozen blocks out of the fjords. And while they're surrounded by unparalleled beauty, from the snow-covered mountains to the dancing northern lights, the icy cold lends a significant element of danger to their awe-inspiring work. After their long day splitting the ice, Burning Love (*brennende kjærlighet*) would offer the ideal incentive to hurry home for a hearty meal. This creamy dish of mashed potatoes is smothered in toppings that range from crispy bacon to pickled beets. Whether striking the ice for love or fear, Kristoff would certainly agree that Burning Love would make a well-loved staple in any harvester's home!

**POTATOES:**

2½ pounds starchy potatoes, such as russets, peeled and cut into cubes

Salt

½ cup milk

1 stick (8 tablespoons) butter, cut into cubes

Pepper

**TOPPING:**

6 slices bacon, chopped into ¾-inch pieces

1 large yellow onion, chopped

8 ounces cremini or button mushrooms, thinly sliced

Salt

3 green onions, sliced, for garnish

Fresh chopped parsley, for garnish

Pickled beets, for serving

1. **TO MAKE THE POTATOES:** In a medium pot over medium-high heat, boil the potatoes in salted water until fork-tender, about 20 minutes. Drain the water and mash the potatoes. Add the milk and butter and continue to mash until the butter is mashed and the potatoes are lump-free. Add salt and pepper to taste.

2. **TO MAKE THE TOPPING:** In a large skillet over medium-high heat, fry the bacon until crisp, then remove and set aside. Pour all but 1 to 2 tablespoons of the grease out of the pan. Add the onion and sauté until translucent and just barely golden, about 5 minutes, then add the mushrooms and continue to sauté until the mushrooms are tender and golden, about 7 minutes. Season with salt.

3. To serve, transfer the mashed potatoes to a serving dish and top with the mushrooms and onions. Sprinkle the bacon over this, followed by the green onions and parsley. Serve with pickled beets on the side.

# "LOST IN THE WOODS" JUNIPER-SCENTED PORK CHOPS WITH MORELS AND PEAS

As Anna follows Elsa on her quest through the Enchanted Forest, Kristoff wonders whether he and his adventurous princess might be growing apart. His elaborate proposal—which involves both fluttery seed pods *and* reindeer!—is thwarted when Anna takes off without telling him, leaving Kristoff feeling as if he's lost in the woods. "Lost in the Woods" Juniper-Scented Pork Chops is a succulent, savory dish imbued with the flavors of a Scandinavian forest. With fresh peas and juniper berries, it evokes the ingredients Kristoff might have spotted during his time with the Northuldra. Tender, buttery, and served alongside crisp pea vines, these chops make the perfect meal to serve to your feisty, fearless, ginger-sweet love . . . or to anyone ready to embark on an epicurean adventure!

**PORK:**

6 pork chops, about 1-inch thick

1 tablespoon kosher salt

1 tablespoon juniper berries, crushed in a mortar and pestle

1 tablespoon butter

**MUSHROOM SAUCE:**

4 tablespoons butter, divided

¼ pound morel mushrooms, washed, trimmed, and cut in half lengthwise (see note)

1 tablespoon chopped shallot

Salt

1 tablespoon flour

2 cups low-sodium chicken broth

**FOR THE PEAS AND PEA VINES:**

1 tablespoon extra-virgin olive oil

1 cup peas, fresh or frozen (defrosted if using frozen)

¼ pound pea vines

Salt

**SPECIALTY TOOLS:**

Mortar and pestle

Kitchen thermometer

1. **TO MAKE THE PORK:** Rub the pork chops on both sides with the salt and crushed juniper berries, pressing in the juniper. Place on a baking sheet and let sit at room temperature for about 30 minutes.

2. Melt the butter in a large skillet over medium-high heat and add the pork chops. Cook until they begin to turn golden, about 4 minutes, then flip and do the same for the other side. Continue to cook, flipping occasionally, until the pork chops reach an internal temperature of 145°F. Remove from the pan and tent with a sheet of aluminum foil to keep the chops warm. Reserve the pan.

3. **TO MAKE THE MUSHROOM SAUCE:** Melt 1 tablespoon butter in a medium pan over medium heat and add the mushrooms, cooking until they begin to soften. Add the chopped shallot and a bit of salt to taste. Remove from the heat.

4. In the pan you used to cook the pork chops, melt the remaining 3 tablespoons butter over medium-high heat. Add the flour and whisk until smooth. Add the chicken broth, a little at a time, whisking constantly, until it thickens and you have a consistency that sticks to the back of a spoon—you may or may not need all of the chicken broth. Add the morels and stir. Season to taste with additional salt if necessary.

5.  **TO MAKE THE PEAS AND PEA VINES:** In a small pan over medium heat, heat the olive oil until it glistens. Add the peas and heat for 1 minute, then add the pea vines. Stir frequently for about 1 minute, until the pea vines begin to wilt but still retain some structure. Season to taste with salt and remove from the heat.

6.  To serve, divide the pork chops among six plates. Spoon the morel sauce over each and serve the peas and pea vines on the side.

**NOTE:** If you're unable to find fresh morels, simply choose another variety of wild mushroom and adjust the cooking time as needed.

# ROASTED PORK WITH CHERRY SAUCE

When autumn dawns, Elsa, Anna, Kristoff, Sven, and Olaf gather together for a delicious harvest feast. They're surrounded by a cornucopia of cuisine—from poultry to potatoes to a positively robust roast! This Roasted Pork with Cherry Sauce would have looked right at home on the royal table. Inspired by *ribbe*—a celebratory Norwegian meal—this version is served alongside a subtly spiced cherry sauce. With tangy jelly and sprigs of thyme, this savory pork roast is sure to connect both lands and people . . . through the love of good food!

**PORK:**

One 3- to 4-pound *ribbe* pork belly with skin
Salt

**CHERRY SAUCE:**

1 cup pitted cherries
½ cup water
¼ cup red current or cherry jelly
2 tablespoons sugar
1 cinnamon stick
teaspoon ground allspice
¼ teaspoon salt, plus more as needed
2 sprigs thyme
2 tablespoons cornstarch, for thickening
1 tablespoon water, plus more as needed
Pepper

**SPECIALTY TOOL:**

Kitchen thermometer

1. **TO MAKE THE PORK:** Preheat the oven to 400°F.

2. Use a sharp knife to score the skin of the pork belly in a crosshatch or diamond pattern all the way into the fat without cutting into the meat. Dry the skin with a paper towel, then sprinkle generously with salt, making sure to get salt into the cuts. Season the rest of the meat with salt, too. Place the pork, skin side up, on a rack in a roasting pan. (If you have time, you can season the pork in advance and let it rest, uncovered, in the fridge for 1 day to allow the skin to dry further, helping it to become crispy.)

3. Place the pork in the oven and roast until the internal temperature reads 145°F. Increase the temperature to 475°F if the crackling needs more time, watching carefully so it doesn't burn.

4. **TO MAKE THE CHERRY SAUCE:** While the pork is cooking, prepare the cherry sauce: In a saucepan, combine the cherries, water, jelly, sugar, cinnamon stick, allspice, salt, and thyme and simmer over medium heat for about 15 minutes. Remove the cinnamon stick and thyme sprigs. In a small bowl, mix the cornstarch with 1 tablespoon or so of water to create a slurry. Stir this into the sauce and simmer another few minutes to thicken the sauce. Season with salt and pepper to taste.

5. When the pork is done, remove it from the oven and let it rest for 15 minutes, then carve and serve with the cherry sauce.

# A THOUSAND REASONS MEATBALLS

There are plenty of reasons for Elsa to ignore the lyrical voice she hears inside her head—a thousand, to be precise. But there's not a single one for her to turn away from these marvelous meatballs. Based on the classic Swedish dish, A Thousand Reasons Meatballs blend beef, pork, and veal into savory orbs of rich flavors. Seasoned with nutmeg and served alongside boiled potatoes and lingonberry jam, this popular Nordic dish will please countless palates!

**MEATBALLS:**

2 tablespoons butter, plus more for cooking the meatballs

1 white or yellow onion, finely chopped

1 pound ground beef

1 pound ground pork

½ pound ground veal

¼ cup flour

½ cup beef broth

2½ teaspoons salt

¼ teaspoon ground allspice

¼ teaspoon ground nutmeg

¼ teaspoon ground white pepper

**BROWN SAUCE:**

2½ cups beef broth

3 tablespoons butter

3 tablespoons flour

1 tablespoon fresh thyme leaves

½ teaspoon salt, plus more as needed

Boiled potatoes, for serving

Lingonberry jam, for serving

1. **TO MAKE THE MEATBALLS:** In a large pan over medium-high heat, heat the butter. Add the onion and sauté until translucent, 5 to 7 minutes. Transfer to a large mixing bowl and combine with the ground beef, ground pork, ground veal, flour, beef broth, salt, allspice, nutmeg, and white pepper, mixing gently to incorporate everything and taking care to not overwork. Chill for about 30 minutes.

2. Shape the meat into balls about 1½ inches in diameter. (Working with damp hands helps keep the meat from sticking.)

3. Using the same pan as before, melt about 1 tablespoon additional butter over medium heat. Pan-fry the meatballs, working in batches, until they're brown on all sides, about 4 minutes per side. Transfer to a platter.

4. **TO MAKE THE SAUCE:** Deglaze the pan with some of the broth, scraping up the pan drippings. Add the rest of the broth, then increase the heat to medium-high to bring to a simmer.

5. In a medium pot, melt the butter over medium heat. Add the flour and whisk constantly until smooth. Add the heated broth about ½ cup at a time, whisking constantly, until you have a gravy that's thick enough to coat a spoon. Stir in the thyme and season with salt to taste.

6. Return the meatballs to the original pan and pour the sauce over them. Simmer over medium heat until cooked through.

7. Serve with boiled potatoes and lingonberry jam.

NOTE: If veal isn't easily accessible, use ground chicken instead.

# STEAK WITH CREAMY WILD MUSHROOMS

Scandinavian summers offer up an abundance of nature-bound activities—from enjoying the hum of the buzzing bees to pulling fluffy strands of dandelion fuzz, taking magnificent hikes, and, of course, foraging for both berries *and* mushrooms. This recipe calls to mind a favorite outdoor pastime while summoning the spirit of the Enchanted Forest—where mushrooms no doubt pepper the ground. Steak with Creamy Wild Mushrooms sears thick steaks atop a cast-iron pan, then tops them off with juniper-seasoned mushrooms. Rich, tangy, and enthusiastically earthy, this robust meal makes for a delightful summertime dish.

**STEAK:**

2 pounds tri-tip steaks (see note)
Salt
2 tablespoons butter

**SAUCE:**

1 cup beef broth
1 tablespoon dried juniper berries, crushed in a mortar and pestle or with the side of a knife
4 thyme sprigs

1 pound wild mushrooms (cremini will work in a pinch)
⅓ cup whipping cream
2 tablespoons freshly squeezed lemon juice
2 teaspoons Worcestershire sauce
1 tablespoon tomato paste

1. **TO MAKE THE STEAK:** Pat the steaks dry and season with salt on all sides. In a large cast-iron pan roomy enough to hold the steaks without overcrowding, melt the butter over medium-high heat. Add the steaks and sear, turning as needed until all sides are deeply browned, about 15 minutes total, then lower the temperature to medium and continue to cooking until the steak reaches the desired temperature. (See chart below for temperatures.)

   - Rare: 120°F–125°F
   - Medium rare: 130°F–135°F
   - Medium: 140°F–145°F
   - Medium well: 150°F–155°F
   - Well done: 160°F and above

2. Transfer the steaks to a plate and cover with aluminum foil to keep warm while you make the sauce.

3. **TO MAKE THE SAUCE:** Return the pan with its drippings to medium-high heat. Pour in the beef broth and add the juniper and thyme, scraping the bottom with a wooden spoon to loosen any bits that stick to the bottom. Simmer for 1 to 2 minutes while you roughly chop the mushrooms. Add the mushrooms and continue to simmer until they're almost tender, 3 to 4 minutes, depending on how delicate the variety is you're using. Add the cream and continue to simmer, stirring regularly, for another minute, until it's slightly thickened and the mushrooms are tender. Stir in the lemon juice, Worcestershire sauce, and tomato paste. Taste and adjust the seasonings as needed.

4. Serve the steaks with the mushrooms on top.

5. Serve with the "Certain Certainties" Butter-Braised Red Potatoes (page 37).

> **NOTES:** Tri-tip is sometimes sold as tri-tip roast, which you can cut down to steaks for this recipe. If you don't have access to tri-tip steak, choose a cut such as sirloin.
>
> Tri-tip steak is from the bottom sirloin of a steer and is a lean cut. I prefer this cooked medium to keep it tender because it's so lean. The rich sauce is a perfect complement.

# CORONATION DAY HERB-CRUSTED PRIME RIB WITH BLUEBERRY AU JUS AND HORSERADISH SAUCE

Anna's coronation is a highly anticipated event. Arendelle has waited years to officially welcome their energetic queen … who wants nothing more than to give her all to her beloved home. Such a momentous occasion is deserving of a truly royal feast, and Coronation Day Herb-Crusted Prime Rib would make for an ideal meal. With a thick cut of meat seasoned by a medley of herbs, and au jus that tastes of summer blueberries, this dish is truly a meal worth melting for.

**MEAT:**

One 9-pound or 4-rib prime rib (also known as standing rib roast)

2 to 3 tablespoons salt

**HERB RUB:**

1 cup loosely packed parsley leaves (upper stems are okay, too)

¼ cup loosely packed sage leaves

¼ cup loosely packed thyme leaves

2 tablespoons rosemary leaves

4 tablespoons extra-virgin olive oil

¼ teaspoon salt

**HORSERADISH CREAM:**

½ cup freshly grated horseradish

¼ cup sour cream

¼ cup mayonnaise

½ teaspoon salt

½ tablespoon freshly squeezed lemon juice

½ teaspoon Worcestershire sauce

**BLUEBERRY AU JUS:**

¼ cup balsamic vinegar

3 tablespoons flour

1 cup beef broth

2 cups fresh blueberries

3 thyme sprigs

2 tablespoons salt, plus more as needed

**SPECIALTY TOOL:**

Kitchen thermometer

1. **TO PREPARE THE PRIME RIB:** Remove the prime rib from the refrigerator and place it on a roasting pan about 2 hours before roasting. Rub salt all over the surface right away to begin to draw out some moisture.

2. **TO MAKE THE HERB RUB:** Place the parsley, sage, thyme, rosemary, olive oil, and salt in a food processor and whirl until finely chopped. Rub this all over the meat.

3. Preheat the oven to 500°F. Slide the roast into the oven and oven-sear it for 15 minutes. Reduce the heat to 325°F and continue to cook until it's cooked to your liking, an internal temperature of 115°F for rare or 120° to 130°F for medium. Check the temperature from time to time using an instant-read meat thermometer; this should take about 2 hours.

4. **TO MAKE THE HORSERADISH CREAM:** While the meat is roasting, in a medium bowl, stir together the horseradish, sour cream, mayonnaise, salt, lemon juice, and Worcestershire sauce. Give it a taste and adjust the seasonings if necessary. Refrigerate until ready to serve.

5. When the meat is cooked through, transfer to a cutting board and cover with aluminum foil to keep warm while it rests for 15 to 30 minutes.

6. **TO MAKE THE BLUEBERRY AU JUS:** In the meantime, take the lower part of the roasting rack, with all the drippings, and place it on the stove over medium-high heat. Pour in the balsamic vinegar and stir, scraping any bits that may have adhered to the bottom of the pan. Add the flour and broth and whisk constantly until the sauce thickens, about 5 minutes. Add the blueberries and thyme sprigs and continue to stir for about 3 minutes, using the back of a spoon to break down the berries a bit. Season with salt to taste.

7. When ready to serve, carve the prime rib into slices. Serve with the horseradish sauce and blueberry sauce on the side.

**NOTE:** It's generally advised to allow for 1 pound of bone-in prime rib per person, but I've found that when serving such a roast at a large dinner, we usually have so many side dishes and starters that people eat considerably less meat. So, keep in mind the appetites of your guests and what else is on the menu. Of course, leftovers are never a bad thing, and when reheated in the oven, this roast is just as good the next day.

# SAILORS BEEF STEW

As a fjord town, Arendelle sees its fair share of seafaring vessels. Boats of all sizes sail into the kingdom's port, bringing a gaggle of goods... and a surplus of sailors. Based on the Swedish stew *sjömansbiff*, Sailors Beef Stew is a hearty dish that could happily feed a whole seafaring crew. Seared beef and sautéed onions are layered with potatoes and herbs, then cooked in a savory broth. Served with pickled beets and whole-grain mustard, this dish will have diners announcing they're living the dream—just like Olaf!

3 pounds chuck or round beef roast, cut into 1- or 1½-inch pieces

2 teaspoons salt

1 teaspoon pepper

cup flour

2 tablespoons olive oil

2 tablespoons butter

3 large thinly sliced yellow onions

1½ cups beef broth

2 pounds waxy potatoes, such as Yukon Gold or new potatoes, peeled and sliced

6 bay leaves

1 tablespoon fresh thyme leaves

Pickled beets, for serving

Whole-grain mustard, for serving

1. In a large bowl, toss the beef with the salt, pepper, and flour. In a large pan over medium-high heat, heat the olive oil and butter. Working in batches to avoid overcrowding, brown the beef on all sides until deeply golden, a few minutes on each side. Remove the beef from the pan and set aside.

2. In the same pan, reduce the heat to medium and sauté the onions until golden and soft, about 20 minutes. Stir frequently and scrape up the brown bits as you go. Deglaze with the beef broth and set aside.

3. Preheat the oven to 325°F. Lightly butter a 2½-quart casserole dish (with a lid). Layer the potatoes, meat, and onions. Nestle bay leaves and thyme throughout. Pour the remaining liquid over the layers. Cover and place in the oven for 3 to 3½ hours, until the meat and vegetables are cooked through and tender. Gently stir occasionally. Remove the bay leaves.

4. Serve with pickled beets and whole-grain mustard.

CHAPTER FIVE

# DESSERTS

# BROWN BUTTER LEFSE WITH SPICED PEARS AND THYME

As one of Norway's most iconic treats, lefse has a long (and tasty!) history. Originally made with flour, this sweet flatbread took on a new form once potatoes made their way to Norway—though Hardanger lefse remains a popular, flour-based treat. This modern-day recipe blends riced potatoes with cream, butter, sugar, and flour, cooks the dough atop a hot skillet, and tops it off with a flavorful cinnamon-sugar-butter spread. Rolled into logs and served alongside seasoned pears, Brown Butter Lefse with spiced Pears and Thyme might just become the answer to Kristoff's thoughtful query: "I'm here. What do you need?"

**LEFSE:**

2 pounds russet potatoes, peeled and cut into pieces

¼ cup (½ stick) butter

2 tablespoons heavy cream

1 tablespoon sugar

¾ teaspoon salt

1 cup all-purpose flour, plus more for rolling the dough

**SPICED PEARS:**

4 tablespoons butter

4 firm, ripe pears, peeled, cored, and thinly sliced

6 tablespoons brown sugar

1 tablespoon fresh thyme leaves

1 teaspoon ground cinnamon

Butter, at room temperature, for serving

Sugar, for serving

Cinnamon, for serving

1. **TO MAKE THE LEFSE:** In a large pot of boiling, salted water, cook the potatoes until fork-tender. Drain and allow to cool slightly. Press the potatoes through a ricer. Measure 2 cups into a large mixing bowl. Reserve the rest for another use.

2. In a small saucepan over medium heat, melt the butter and continue to heat until the butter turns golden brown and smells nutty, about 3 minutes. Once the milk solids separate, remove it from the heat and pour it into a small bowl, trying to leave the brown bits behind. Add the cream, sugar, and salt to the butter and stir to combine. Pour this over the potatoes and stir to incorporate. Cover and refrigerate for several hours or overnight.

3. Add the flour to the potatoes, using your hands to thoroughly mix the ingredients and smooth out any lumps. Shape the dough into balls a little larger than a golf ball. Flatten them into pucks and refrigerate while setting up your workstation.

4. Preheat a large nonstick skillet over medium-low heat. Generously sprinkle flour over a flat surface, ideally using a cloth-covered pastry board. Rub flour over the surface of a rolling pin, too. (Ideally, you'll have a cloth-covered corrugated one.)

5. Remove a few pucks of dough from the refrigerator. (You want them to stay chilled.) Dip both sides of one into flour and place it on the board, rolling it to make a thin circle.

6. Slide a heatproof spatula under the dough and carefully use it to remove the lefse from the board and transfer it to the skillet. Cook until bubbles start to form on the surface of the lefse and the underside starts to develop some light brown spots. Flip and cook the other side.

7. Transfer to a clean surface and brush off any excess flour. Cover with a clean tea towel while making the rest of the lefse. Repeat with the remaining dough.

8. **TO MAKE THE SPICED PEARS:** In a skillet over medium heat, melt the butter. Add the pear slices and top with the brown sugar, thyme, and cinnamon. Gently sauté for about 5 minutes, until the pears are soft and slightly caramelized.

9. To serve, spread the lefse with butter and sprinkle with sugar and cinnamon. Roll up and cut lengthwise into 1-inch-long pieces, if desired. Serve with the spiced pears.

10. To store, fold each lefse into quarters and wrap in waxed paper and airtight plastic bags. Refrigerate for up to a few days, or freeze for up to 2 months.

# HOMEMADE "DO YOU WANT TO BUILD A SNOWMAN?" ICE CREAM

Growing up, Elsa and Anna loved to build a very specific snowman. They named their creation Olaf and quickly decided that he was fiercely fond of warm hugs. This homemade ice cream calls on the sisters' creative spirit by allowing culinary creators to craft a frosty dessert of their own invention. A sweet, snow-colored base enhanced by delicious birch syrup is covered with grated chocolate and an edible glitter that bears a striking resemblance to Olaf's permafrost. Topped with flowers—like those one might see in summer!—Homemade "Do You Want to Build a Snowman?" Ice Cream will have diners tap-dancing with joy . . . just like their favorite singing snowman!

1 vanilla bean

2 cups heavy cream

1 cup whole milk

1 sprig rosemary

4 large egg yolks

¾ cup sugar

Pinch salt

3 to 4 tablespoons birch syrup

Edible flowers and edible
 glitter, for serving

Grated chocolate, for serving

**SPECIALTY TOOL:**

Ice-cream maker

1. Before you get started, prepare your ice-cream maker according to the manufacturer's instructions; if using an electric one, you may need to freeze the bowl for 24 hours. (See note.)

2. Use the tip of a sharp knife to split the vanilla bean lengthwise. Scrape out the seeds using the back of the knife.

3. In a medium saucepan over medium heat, combine the heavy cream, milk, vanilla bean seeds and pod, and rosemary sprig. Heat until warm but not boiling, stirring occasionally. Once warm, remove from the heat.

4. While the cream mixture is warming, in a mixing bowl, whisk the egg yolks, sugar, and salt until pale and thickened slightly.

5. To temper the eggs, gradually add a small amount of the warm cream into the egg yolks while whisking constantly. Slowly add the remaining warm cream while continuing to constantly whisk.

6. Put the mixture back in the saucepan and place over low heat. Cook, stirring constantly, until it's thick and coats the back of the spoon, without boiling, 5 to 7 minutes. Remove from the heat and strain through a fine-mesh sieve into a clean bowl.

7. Set a sheet of plastic wrap on the custard so it touches the surface of the custard to keep a skin from forming, place it in the refrigerator, and allow to chill completely, at least 4 hours but ideally overnight.

8. Pour the chilled custard into an ice-cream maker and churn using the manufacturer's instructions. When the ice cream is almost complete, at a soft-serve consistency, transfer half to an airtight container. Drizzle the birch syrup over it and top with the remaining half of the ice cream. Use a knife to swirl the birch syrup throughout, taking care to not overmix. Freeze for a few hours to firm up. Remove from the freezer about 10 minutes before serving to soften slightly, making scooping easier. To serve, spoon into bowls or ice-cream cones and decorate with edible flowers, a sprinkle of edible glitter, and dusting of grated chocolate.

**NOTE:** Churning with an ice-cream machine yields the best results, but if you don't have one, transfer the chilled custard to the freezer and stir every 30 minutes for several hours until frozen.

# PERSONAL FLURRY PAVLOVA

Olaf had always dreamed of experiencing the summer, the sun, and all things hot. But the cheery snowman soon discovered that getting too close to heat can be problematic—especially when you're made of snow! Luckily, when the eternal winter ended, Elsa gifted Olaf his own personal flurry, allowing him to remain nice and cool (and solid!). Personal Flurry Pavlova offers a playful nod to that particularly inspired piece of magic. This *hovdessert*—a dessert crafted for the royal court—takes fluffy, white meringue and tops it off with pastry cream and summery fruits. Light, sweet, and seasonally scrumptious, Personal Flurry Pavlova is a true delight, just like Olaf himself!

**PAVLOVA:**

4 egg whites, at room temperature

¾ cup sugar

1 teaspoon cornstarch

½ teaspoon distilled white vinegar

**PASTRY CREAM:**

2 cups whole milk

4 large eggs

½ cup sugar

¼ cup cornstarch

1 teaspoon vanilla extract

2 to 3 ripe white-flesh peaches or nectarines, thinly sliced

Whipped cream, for serving

½ cup shredded coconut

¼ cup sliced almonds

1. **TO MAKE THE PAVLOVA:** Preheat the oven to 300°F. Line a baking sheet with parchment paper. In a large mixing bowl—ideally, using a stand or electric mixer—beat the egg whites until they're frothy. Add the sugar, cornstarch, and vinegar and continue to beat until stiff.

2. Spoon the meringue onto the prepared baking sheet in a circle about 8 inches in diameter. Slide it into the oven and bake until the pavlova is firm and the outside is dry, about 1 hour, but check occasionally. Let cool. This can be made 1 to 2 days in advance.

3. **TO MAKE THE PASTRY CREAM:** Heat the milk in a saucepan over medium heat until it begins to simmer, then remove. In a large mixing bowl, whisk the eggs, sugar, cornstarch, and vanilla until well combined. Slowly add the hot milk, whisking constantly, until smooth and combined. Return to the saucepan and cook over medium heat, stirring constantly, until thick. Remove from the heat, cover with a sheet of plastic wrap, and let cool completely.

4. To assemble, place the cooled pavlova on a serving dish. Spoon the chilled pastry cream over the pavlova and arrange the peaches over top. Garnish with dollops of whipped cream, then sprinkle with the shredded coconut and sliced almonds.

> **NOTE:** This recipe is gluten-free, as long as you choose a gluten-free cornstarch.

# TROLL CREAM

The lovingly loyal Kristoff was raised by trolls. When he and Sven were quite young, Grand Pabbie and his family of rolling relatives took them in—and the now-grown pair continue to circle back whenever they need advice. *Trollkrem* is a whipped lingonberry cream that pays a tasty tribute to Kristoff's found family. Served in a *krumkake* cone or alongside a crispy cookie, Troll Cream will be a hit at any family gathering—rocky or otherwise!

1 cup heavy whipping cream
½ teaspoon sugar
½ cup lingonberry jam (see note)

¼ teaspoon vanilla extract
¼ teaspoon ground cinnamon
⅛ teaspoon freshly ground cardamom

Mint leaves, for garnish
Fresh or frozen lingonberries, for garnish (optional)

1. In a mixing bowl using a stand mixer, if possible, beat the heavy whipping cream and sugar until it reaches stiff peaks, 3 to 5 minutes.

2. Using a spatula, carefully fold in the jam, vanilla, cinnamon, and cardamom. Serve in individual serving dishes or glasses. Garnish with mint leaves and a couple fresh berries.

> **NOTE:** If you can't find lingonberry jam, use another fruit jam, such as raspberry or blackberry, adjusting the sugar as needed.

# SNOW CONE ICE MONSTER

Elsa's frosty monster protects her ice palace, sending intruders—and friendly sisters!—away so the snowy queen can work through her powers in solitude. But the crown-loving Marshmallow finds himself won over by Olaf's dynamic storytelling . . . and a cheerful army of little brothers. Snow Cone Ice Monster is a frosty confection made up to resemble Elsa's sometimes-vigilant guard. With chocolate chip eyes and pretzels for arms, this treat calls to mind the wintry joy of building a snowman. Just remember: "It is not nice to throw people!"

½ cup water
½ cup granulated sugar
½ cup honey
Pinch salt
1 teaspoon vanilla extract

4 cups ice cubes (crushed or shaved)

**SPECIALTY TOOL:**

Shaved-ice machine

White marshmallows, for decorating
Mini chocolate chips, for decorating
Pretzel sticks, for decorating

1. In a medium saucepan over medium heat, combine the water, sugar, honey, and salt. Stir until the sugar and honey dissolve, creating a syrup. Remove the saucepan from the heat. Stir in the vanilla and allow to cool to room temperature, then chill in the refrigerator.

2. Using a typical shaved-ice machine, follow the manufacturer's instructions to shave the ice into a snowlike consistency until you have enough for two servings.

3. To assemble the snow cone monsters, use an ice-cream scoop and spoons to place a large scoop of lightly packed ice in the bottom of two shallow bowls. Shape the ice into heads and limbs. Pour the cooled syrup over the ice monsters, allowing it to coat the ice thoroughly.

4. Add white marshmallows, mini chocolate chips, and pretzel sticks as desired to create added monster shapes, eyes, and limbs.

> **NOTE:** If you don't have a shaved-ice maker, you can pulse crushed ice in a blender or food processor, but this method won't yield the same fluffy results.

# NORTHERN LIGHTS ICE POPS

In the winter, the aurora borealis dances across Scandinavian skies, illuminating the fjords with its special brand of magic. These Northern Lights Ice Pops bring in the colors of that brilliant phenomenon and add an extra bit of sparkle through fun, festive flavors. Butterfly pea flowers create a rich, indigo hue, whereas blackberries and avocado round out the rainbow. Bold, sweet, and as cold as the northern nights, these ice pops are an energizing treat that will fuel hours of fun. After all, when the sky's awake, one *has* to play!

1 tablespoon dried butterfly pea flowers
¼ cup hot water

**YOGURT BASE:**

1 cup vanilla yogurt
½ cup milk
1 tablespoon sugar
1 tablespoon cornstarch

**BERRY SWIRL:**

½ cup blackberries
1 teaspoon granulated sugar
1 teaspoon lemon juice

**AVOCADO LAYER:**

1 ripe extra-large avocado, peeled and roughly chopped
2 tablespoons granulated sugar

¼ cup water
Juice and zest of 1 lime (2 tablespoons juice, 1 tablespoon zest)

**SPECIALTY TOOLS:**

Ice-pop molds
Skewer
Ice-pop sticks

1.  In a small bowl, pour hot water over the dried butterfly pea flowers. Allow to steep for 10 minutes, then strain out the flowers and reserve the water, chilling while you prepare the rest of the recipe.

2.  **TO MAKE THE YOGURT BASE:** In a medium mixing bowl, stir the yogurt, milk, sugar, and cornstarch until smooth and there are no cornstarch lumps. Taste and add more sugar if desired.

3.  **TO MAKE THE BERRY SWIRL:** In a small bowl, mash the berries, sugar, and lemon juice and zest with a fork.

4.  **TO MAKE THE AVOCADO LAYER:** In a food processor, purée the avocado, sugar, and water.

5.  Pour the yogurt base into the ice-pop molds, about one third of the way full each. Add a spoonful of berries in each, followed by a bit of avocado purée. Continue to layer until almost full. Pour the reserved flower water over each and use a skewer to swirl the layers together.

6.  Place ice-pop sticks in the molds and freeze until solid, at least 5 hours.

NOTE: This recipe is gluten-free if using gluten-free cornstarch.

# FRUITS OF THE ENCHANTED FOREST SORBET

During the warmer months, Scandinavian forests are ripe with berries. From blackberries to lingonberries to the elusive cloudberry, these popular fruits season jams, pastries, and, of course, frozen desserts. Fruits of the Enchanted Forest Sorbet brings together the tastes of a Scandinavian summer, combining the sweet and tangy flavors that are adored in Arendelle and beyond.

2 pounds mixed berries (such as blueberries, strawberries, and raspberries), fresh or frozen

1 cup water

1 cup sugar

2 tablespoons dried culinary-grade lavender flowers

2 tablespoons dried elderberries

1 tablespoon dried juniper berries, crushed

½ tablespoon freshly squeezed lemon juice

**SPECIALTY TOOL:**

Ice-cream maker

1. Before you get started, prepare your ice-cream maker according to the manufacturer's instructions; if using an electric one, you may need to freeze the bowl for 24 hours. (See note.)

2. If you're using frozen berries, allow these to defrost before using.

3. In a saucepan over high heat, combine the water, sugar, lavender flowers, elderberries, and juniper berries and bring to a boil. Lower the heat to medium and simmer until the sugar is dissolved, about 5 minutes. Remove from the heat and allow the lavender, elderberries, and juniper to steep while the syrup cools. After about 30 minutes, strain through a fine-mesh sieve into a jar to remove the solids. Refrigerate the syrup until cold and retain the berries.

4. In a blender, combine the berries and some of the cooled simple syrup. Blend until liquefied. Strain the juice to remove the seeds (optional). Stir in the lemon juice. Chill for at least 1 hour.

5. Churn the sorbet according to the manufacturer's instructions, about 20 minutes, until thickened. Transfer to containers, cover, and freeze at least 4 hours. Remove from the freezer about 10 minutes before serving to soften slightly, making scooping easier.

> **NOTE:** If you don't have an ice-cream maker, transfer the sorbet to the freezer and stir every 30 minutes for several hours, breaking up any ice crystals, until firm.

# "SPLIT THE ICE APART" PANNA COTTA

Ice mining can be a tricky business. Not only does it require long hours laboring through dark polar nights, but the frosty temperatures—and slippery conditions!—make this job a decidedly daring vocation. After a long session of ice carving, miners deserve a celebration—and this panna cotta would be sure to hit the mark. With sweetened cream coated in a clear candy shell that can be cracked like the frigid fjords, "Split the Ice Apart" Panna Cotta is one frozen heart that's all beauty—no danger.

**PANNA COTTA:**

1 packet unflavored gelatin (2¼ teaspoons)
3 tablespoons cold water
2 cups heavy cream

½ cup whole milk
½ cup granulated sugar
4 ounces white chocolate, finely chopped
2 teaspoons vanilla extract

**TOPPING:**

Precooked isomalt pieces (see note)
White or pearl-colored edible luster dust

1. **TO MAKE THE PANNA COTTA:** In a small bowl, sprinkle the gelatin over the cold water, letting it sit until it softens, 5 to 10 minutes.

2. Meanwhile, in a saucepan over medium heat, combine the cream, milk, and sugar and stir constantly until it just begins to simmer. Remove from the heat. Stir in the white chocolate, vanilla, and prepared gelatin until the chocolate melts and the gelatin dissolves.

3. Pour into 6 to 8 ramekins. Cover with plastic wrap and refrigerate until completely set, at least 4 hours or overnight.

4. **TO MAKE THE TOPPING:** Place the isomalt pieces in a microwave-safe bowl and microwave for 30 seconds, then at 15-second intervals if needed, stirring each time, until melted. Allow to cool, but not so much that it hardens before you can pour it. Pour an even layer over each panna cotta and allow to harden. Sprinkle edible luster dust in a decorative design on the surface of the panna cotta (such as sprinkling ½ teaspoon on one end and then tipping the ramekin and tapping it to scatter the dust down the surface, giving it an ombré, or shaded, effect).

5. Serve immediately.

> **NOTES:** It's important to use precooked isomalt rather than the raw crystals.
>
> This recipe is gluten-free as long as the specific ingredients are gluten-free.

# ICE PALACE KRANSEKAKE

*Kransekake*—a traditional Norwegian wreath cake—is a staple in Arendelle. Featured in Olaf's yuletide shenanigans and during Anna's whistling walk through town, this much-loved dish features prominently throughout the kingdom. This version, Ice Palace Kransekake, brings the classic Nordic cake into homes around the world. With almond flour, confectioner's sugar, and fresh cardamom baked into ring-shaped pans and stacked into a tall tower, this elegant cake is a true work of art. Decorated with icing and sprinkled with edible glitter, this *kransekake* is sure to bring a touch of magic to any celebration—happy, merry, or otherwise!

**DOUGH:**

1½ pounds almond flour

1½ pounds confectioners' sugar

1 tablespoon freshly grated orange zest

½ teaspoon freshly ground cardamom

4 egg whites, lightly beaten

1 teaspoon almond extract

Baking spray or neutral oil, for greasing the molds

Semolina or cornmeal, for dusting the molds

**ICING:**

1 pound confectioners' sugar

3 egg whites, lightly beaten

1 tablespoon lemon juice

White edible glitter, for decorating

Candy pearls, for decorating

**SPECIALTY TOOLS:**

*Kransekake* ring molds

Pastry bag with small tip

1. **TO MAKE THE DOUGH:** Preheat the oven to 350°F.

2. In a large mixing bowl, combine the almond flour, confectioners' sugar, orange zest, and cardamom. Slowly add the egg whites and almond extract while mixing to form a smooth dough. Cover the bowl with plastic wrap and chill in the refrigerator overnight.

3. Spray the molds with a baking spray or brush with a neutral oil, then dust with semolina or cornmeal. Roll small portions of dough into finger-width ropes and press into the prepared molds.

4. Place the molds on baking sheets and bake for about 10 minutes, or until light gold. (Rotate the molds, if necessary, for even baking.) Let cool for 10 minutes before removing from the molds and finish cooling on a wire rack. At this point, the rings can be refrigerated or even frozen, which enhances the texture.

5. **TO MAKE THE ICING:** In a medium bowl, whisk together the confectioners' sugar, egg whites, and lemon juice until smooth and thick. Transfer this to pastry bag with a small tip.

6. To assemble the *kransekake*, place the largest ring on a serving plate or cake stand. Affix the next-largest one to this using icing, also piping the icing over it in a decorative manner, and sprinkling on the edible glitter and candy pearls before attaching the next layer. Repeat until all the rings are used, forming a beautiful towering cake reminiscent of a castle.

7. When it's time to serve, remove the bottom ring, breaking off pieces, working your way up as you go.

**NOTE:** This recipe is easily made gluten-free by using cornmeal to dust the molds.

# CORONATION DAY PRINCESS CAKE

Sweden's classic princess cake is a delightful, dome-shaped dessert. Traditionally covered in green marzipan and topped with a pink rose, this treat was created in the early twentieth century . . . and was so loved by Sweden's young princesses that the *Grön Tårta* (green cake) was renamed for them! This modern-day recipe layers a delicate sponge cake with raspberry jam and cream before topping everything off with a covering of mint-colored marzipan. With rich pastry cream and flavorful fillings, Coronation Day Princess Cake would make a delightful dessert for a pair of Arendellian princesses . . . and anyone who's feeling a bit royal!

**CAKE:**

Nonstick baking spray

6 eggs, separated

1 cup sugar

½ teaspoon cream of tartar

1 teaspoon vanilla extract

1 cup cake flour

1 teaspoon baking powder

¼ teaspoon salt

**PASTRY CREAM:**

2 cups whole milk

4 large eggs

½ cup sugar

¼ cup cornstarch

1 teaspoon vanilla extract

1 packet unflavored gelatin

**WHIPPED CREAM:**

1½ cups heavy whipping cream

3 tablespoons confectioners' sugar

**FILLING AND TOPPING:**

½ cup raspberry jam

14 ounces marzipan

Green and pink food coloring, or color of your choice

Confectioners' sugar or cornstarch, for dusting

Ribbon or candy pearls

1. **TO MAKE THE CAKE:** Preheat the oven to 325°F. Line a 9-inch springform pan with a circle of parchment paper. Coat with nonstick baking spray.

2. In a large mixing bowl, beat the egg whites, sugar, and cream of tartar until pale and fluffy, about 6 minutes. Stir in the vanilla. In a separate bowl, beat the egg yolks until mixed. In a third bowl, mix the cake flour, baking powder, and salt, then stir in the egg yolks until batter is smooth. Gently fold the egg white mixture into the batter. Pour the batter into the pan.

3. Bake until the center springs back when you touch it, about 45 minutes. Cool on a wire rack, then remove from the pan.

4. **TO MAKE THE PASTRY CREAM:** Heat the milk in a saucepan over medium heat until it begins to simmer, then remove from the heat. In a separate mixing bowl, whisk the eggs, sugar, cornstarch, and vanilla until well combined. Slowly pour the hot milk into this mixture, whisking constantly, until smooth and combined.

5. Return the mixture to the saucepan and cook over medium heat, stirring constantly, until thick. Stir in the gelatin until dissolved. Remove from the heat and let cool completely.

6. **TO MAKE THE WHIPPED CREAM:** In a large bowl, beat the cream and sugar with an electric mixer until soft peaks form. Fold this mixture into the pastry cream until smooth.

7. To assemble the cake, slice it into three horizontal layers using a long serrated knife. Place the bottom layer on a cake stand. Spread with about one-quarter of the pastry cream, then place the second layer on top. Cover this layer with raspberry jam and another one-quarter of the pastry cream. Place the final layer of cake on top of this one. Coat the sides of the cake with additional pastry cream and generously pile the remainder of the pastry cream on top into a dome.

8. Knead the marzipan (reserving a little bit) and food coloring until the marzipan is a minty green. Knead the reserved marzipan with the pink food coloring to form a rose to top the cake, if you'd like. Cut out three 1-inch circles, fold them in half, lay them down overlapping slightly, and roll up tightly to make the rose center. Cut out five more circles, cut them in half, lay down five halves, overlapping slightly, and roll these "petals" around the center. Continue with the remaining halves, or more, until the rose is as full as you want. Powdered sugar or cornstarch dusted on the marzipan can help prevent sticking while working to create the rose. Roll out the green marzipan on a surface dusted lightly with confectioners' sugar. It should be about ⅛-inch thick. Drape over the cake and trim away any excess marzipan with a sharp knife.

9. Dust with confectioners' sugar and top with the marzipan rose, if you make one. Line the bottom of the cake with a ribbon or candy pearls to cover any unevenness of the marzipan.

# FIXER-UPPER CARROT CAKE

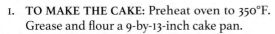

It's no secret that Sven loves his carrots: The loyal reindeer perks up when Anna buys him a batch, and he nips at Olaf's new nose upon meeting the chatty snowman. So, if ever Sven were to bake a cake to celebrate his best friend's long-awaited engagement, his chosen confection would no doubt incorporate carrots. Fixer-Upper Carrot Cake is an impeccable imagining of Sven's dream dessert. Two cups of carrots are baked into a light, fluffy dough, then topped with cream cheese frosting. With tangy lemon juice and just a hint of cardamom, this cake would leave a certain couple—and their carrot-loving friend—singing in happy harmony!

**CAKE:**

1 cup canola oil, plus more for greasing

2 cups all-purpose flour, plus more for dusting the cake pan

1 cup granulated sugar

⅓ cup packed brown sugar

4 large eggs

2 teaspoons baking powder

2 teaspoons baking soda

2 teaspoons ground cinnamon

1 teaspoon ground cardamom

½ teaspoon ground ginger

½ teaspoon salt

2 cups grated carrots (about 4 carrots)

2 tablespoons lemon juice

1 teaspoon vanilla extract

**FROSTING:**

8 ounces cream cheese, room temperature

1 stick butter, at room temperature

4 cups confectioners' sugar

1 teaspoon vanilla extract

½ teaspoon almond extract

Finely grated zest of 1 lemon

1. **TO MAKE THE CAKE:** Preheat oven to 350°F. Grease and flour a 9-by-13-inch cake pan.

2. In a large mixing bowl, beat the granulated sugar, brown sugar, and oil together until smooth, then add the eggs, one at a time, beating in between each addition.

3. Tip the flour into the mixing bowl and add the baking powder, baking soda, cinnamon, cardamom, ginger, and salt. Lightly beat until just incorporated. Add the carrots, lemon juice, and vanilla and stir to combine.

4. Pour into the prepared cake pan and bake for 35 to 40 minutes, until a toothpick comes out clean. Let cool in the pan.

5. **TO MAKE THE FROSTING:** In a large mixing bowl, beat the cream cheese and butter to combine, then add the confectioners' sugar and continue beating until creamy and smooth. Stir in the vanilla and almond extracts. Spread the frosting over the cooled cake and sprinkle with lemon zest.

# THAW THE WINTER CAKE

When Elsa accidentally freezes the fjord (along with the entire region!), Anna lets her know that things will be OK . . . she can just unfreeze it! But figuring out how to thaw an eternal winter *everywhere* can take some time. And such a formidable feat would surely require a solid dose of energy. Thaw the Winter Cake—a modern twist on the classic Norwegian *bløtkake*—is a sublimely sweet treat for anyone about to undertake an enormous task. Chocolate sponge cake is layered with blueberry jam and vanilla pastry cream, then topped off with a buttercream frosting. Sprinkled with grated chocolate and decorated with edible glitter and flowers, this elegant cake invokes the spirit of the great outdoors . . . and its snowy queen!

**CAKE:**

Nonstick baking spray

2 cups all-purpose flour

2 cups granulated sugar

½ cup unsweetened cocoa powder

2 teaspoons baking soda

1 teaspoon baking powder

1 teaspoon salt

1 teaspoon instant espresso powder

1 cup buttermilk

2 large eggs, at room temperature

½ cup vegetable oil

2 teaspoon vanilla extract

1 cup hot water

**PASTRY CREAM:**

2 cups whole milk

3 eggs

½ cup granulated sugar

3 tablespoons cornstarch

1 teaspoon vanilla extract

teaspoon salt

1 tablespoon butter

1 cup blueberry jam, excess liquid strained if loose

**BUTTERCREAM:**

2 sticks unsalted butter, at room temperature

4 cups confectioners' sugar, sifted

2 teaspoons clear vanilla extract

2 to 4 tablespoons heavy cream

Bright white color gel

Violet color gel

Finely grated chocolate, for decorating

White edible flowers, for decorating

White edible glitter and pearls, for decorating

1. **TO MAKE THE CAKE:** Preheat the oven to 350°F. Spray two 9-inch round cake pans with nonstick baking spray. In a large mixing bowl, whisk together the flour, sugar, cocoa powder, baking soda, baking powder, salt, and instant espresso powder to combine.

2. In a separate large mixing bowl, whisk the buttermilk, eggs, vegetable oil, and vanilla until thoroughly combined. Tip in the dry ingredients and stir to combine. Slowly pour in the hot water.

3. Divide the batter evenly between the two prepared pans and bake for 25 to 30 minutes, until a toothpick inserted in the middle comes out clean. Cool on a wire rack.

4. **TO MAKE THE PASTRY CREAM:** Heat the milk in a medium saucepan over medium heat until it begins to simmer, then remove from the heat. In a large mixing bowl, vigorously whisk the eggs, sugar, cornstarch, vanilla, and salt until well combined. Slowly pour the hot milk into this mixture, whisking constantly, until smooth and combined.

5. Return to the saucepan and cook over medium heat, stirring constantly, until thick. Remove from the heat and place the saucepan in an ice bath. Add the butter and stir until the butter melts. Let cool completely.

6. **TO MAKE THE BUTTERCREAM:** Using a stand mixer, whip the butter until creamy and light in color. Sift the confectioners' sugar and gradually mix it into the butter, mixing on low speed until completely incorporated. Add the clear vanilla. Increase mixing speed to medium and continue to whip for a couple of minutes. Slowly add the cream until you have a spreadable consistency. To make the buttercream whiter, use a little bright white color gel and just a touch of violet color to neutralize the yellow.

7. To assemble the cake, place one layer on a cake stand. Spread the blueberry jam over this cake layer, then add a layer of pastry cream. Top with the second cake layer. Frost the cake with the buttercream.

8. Lightly dust the top with grated chocolate to mimic dirt and decorate with white edible flowers and edible glitter to resemble snow.

# "WHAT'S THAT AMAZING SMELL?" CHOCOLATE TORTE

Anna and Elsa simply adore chocolate. From cakes to fountains to cocoa, the sisters have enjoyed countless helpings of this flavorful food. "What's That Amazing Smell?" Chocolate Torte recalls the touching moment from Elsa's coronation when the sisters noticed an especially scintillating smell . . . and shared their appreciation for all things chocolate. Based on Sweden's *kladdkaka* and cooked to gooey perfection, this sweet cocoa-filled torte is bound to bring the entire kingdom to the table!

1 cup (2 sticks) unsalted butter, plus more for greasing

8 ounces bittersweet chocolate, roughly chopped

1 teaspoon instant espresso powder

1 teaspoon vanilla extract

4 eggs

1 cup granulated sugar

¾ cup all-purpose flour

¼ cup rye flour

¼ cup unsweetened cocoa powder

⅛ teaspoon salt

Confectioners' sugar

1. Preheat the oven to 350°F.

2. Grease a 9-inch round cake pan with butter or nonstick cooking spray and line it with parchment paper.

3. In a saucepan over medium heat, melt the butter, then remove from the heat and add the chocolate, stirring until melted. Add the espresso powder and vanilla and stir until smooth. Set aside to cool slightly.

4. In a large mixing bowl, whisk the eggs and granulated sugar until combined. Gradually add the melted chocolate and butter, whisking constantly.

5. In a medium mixing bowl, whisk together the all-purpose flour, rye flour, cocoa powder, and salt. Gradually add to the batter. Pour into the pan.

6. Bake for 25 to 30 minutes, until the edges are set and the center just barely jiggles. Cool in the pan for about 30 minutes to allow the cake to continue setting.

7. Dust with confectioners' sugar, using a stencil to create an intricate design, if desired.

# FROZEN FRACTALS GINGERSNAPS

Ginger cookies play a large role in Scandinavian baking. This popular Christmastime treat is believed to have arrived in Sweden in the 1300s and has since been incorporated into gingerbread cookies, gingerbread houses, and the beloved *pepparkaker*—gingersnaps! This recipe draws inspiration from the cookies of old while invoking the shapes of Elsa's icy evolution. With cinnamon, cardamom, and the ever-popular ginger, Frozen Fractals Gingersnaps are a suitable snack to set out in the midst of a raging storm, during a cheerful gathering, or simply when redecorating one's nearest, northernmost mountain. They're so delicious, you won't want to let them go!

⅓ cup butter

⅓ cup sugar

¼ cup molasses

2 tablespoons heavy cream

1½ teaspoons ground cinnamon

¾ teaspoon freshly ground cardamom

¾ teaspoon ground cloves

¾ teaspoon ground ginger

1½ cups flour, plus more for dusting the work surface

½ teaspoon baking soda

Clear precooked isomalt pieces (see note)

**SPECIALTY TOOLS:**

2 diamond-shaped cookie cutters, one smaller than the other

1. In a medium saucepan over medium-low heat, mix the butter, sugar, and molasses until the butter melts and the sugar dissolves. Allow to cool for a few minutes, then stir in the cream, cinnamon, cardamom, cloves, and ginger.

2. In a large mixing bowl, whisk together the flour and baking soda. Add the butter mixture and stir until the ingredients are well combined and a dough is formed. Divide into two equal portions, wrap each in plastic wrap, and refrigerate overnight.

3. Preheat the oven to 350°F. Line two baking sheets with parchment paper. On a lightly floured surface, roll out a handful of the dough very thin, about ¼-inch thick. Keep the other dough portions in the refrigerator, as working with cold dough makes it easier to handle.

4. Using the diamond-shaped cookie cutter, cut the dough into the shapes of your choice, using a smaller cutter to create windows or openings in the center, and transfer to the prepared baking sheets.

5. Bake one tray at a time for about 10 minutes, until the edges are barely starting to turn color and the candy has melted. Cool on the baking sheet for 5 minutes. In a microwave-safe bowl, place the precooked isomalt pieces and microwave for 30 seconds, then at 15-second intervals if needed, stirring each time, until melted. Allow to cool slightly, then pour into the windows of the cookies. Allow to harden, then transfer to a wire rack. When cool, store in an airtight container for up to 2 to 3 weeks.

**NOTES:** It's important to use precooked isomalt rather than the raw crystals.

This recipe is easily made gluten-free if made with your favorite gluten-free flour blend.

# ICE MINERS SUGAR COOKIES

*Kakemenn*—Norwegian cake men—are a traditional Nordic treat. They pair well with cocoa or coffee and can be easily transported for sharing with a friend . . . or neighboring castle! Ice Miners Sugar Cookies offer an icy twist on this beloved classic. This recipe takes traditional sugar cookies—a nod to Olaf's newly discovered wavy Norway-shaped treat—and molds them into the shape of the ice carvers who work beneath the aurora borealis. Born not of cold ice but of lovingly crafted dough, these delectable miners will be the hit of any event—from birthdays to coronations to any party that happens to be thrown at *that* time of year!

1½ cups granulated sugar

¾ cup milk

1 stick (½ cup) salted butter, melted

2 teaspoons vanilla extract

4 cups all-purpose flour

1 teaspoon baking soda

Marshmallow cream, for decorating

Ground cinnamon, for decorating

Color icing gel, for decorating

**SPECIALTY TOOL:**

Person-shaped cookie cutter

1. In a large mixing bowl, combine the sugar, milk, butter, and vanilla. Add the flour and baking soda and beat until the ingredients are fully incorporated and form a dough. Wrap and chill the dough for several hours or overnight.

2. Preheat the oven to 350°F and line two baking sheets with parchment paper. On a lightly floured surface, roll out the dough to about ¼-inch thick. Using a cookie cutter, cut out shapes and transfer to the prepared baking sheets, spacing them about 1½ inches apart.

3. Bake for about 10 minutes, until the edges start to crisp. (The centers will still be somewhat soft.) Transfer to a baking rack to cool completely.

4. To decorate, spread the marshmallow cream over the top of each cookie, almost to the edge. Sprinkle with cinnamon. Draw on a face with the gel.

5. Store refrigerated in airtight container for up to 2 weeks.

# "SHOVE SOME CHOCOLATE IN MY FACE" MARZIPAN TRUFFLES

Elsa's coronation offers Anna the chance to *finally* meet some real-life people from outside the castle walls . . . and indulge in her love of sweets! This no-bake delicacy invokes one of her all-time favorite flavors: chocolate. "Shove Some Chocolate in My Face" Marzipan Truffles are easy to prepare, making them an ideal treat for adults and children to make together. Almond meal and confectioners' sugar are mixed with sweet seasonings, coated with chocolate, and decorated with sprinkles and almonds. Fun to create and even more enjoyable to eat, these chocolaty truffles are so delicious that parents, kids, and chocolate-loving princesses might even be tempted to shove them in their faces!

**MARZIPAN:**

2 cups almond meal
1 cup confectioners' sugar
4 tablespoons corn syrup
1 teaspoon almond extract
1 teaspoon vanilla extract
1 teaspoon orange zest

1 tablespoon water (optional)
12 to 24 red glacé cherries

**CHOCOLATE COATING:**

7 ounces bittersweet
  chocolate, chopped
1 to 2 teaspoons vegetable oil

**FOR DECORATING:**

Sprinkles in various colors
Sliced almonds

1.  **TO MAKE THE MARZIPAN:** Line a baking sheet with parchment paper. In a food processor, combine the almond meal and confectioners' sugar. Add the corn syrup, almond and vanilla extracts, and orange zest and pulse until a thick dough forms, scraping down the sides as necessary. (Add 1 tablespoon water, if needed, to create a smooth dough.) Take some of the marzipan dough and form into balls about ¾ inch in diameter. Use some of the remaining dough to wrap marzipan around the cherries, creating balls the same size as the original. Set these on the prepared baking sheet and chill for 30 minutes while you make the chocolate coating.

2.  **TO MAKE THE CHOCOLATE COATING:** Melt half of the chopped chocolate in a double boiler. Remove the bowl from the heat and stir in the vegetable oil and the other half of the chocolate. Stir until melted and smooth. Let cool slightly.

3.  Use a dipping tool or fork to dip each marzipan ball into the melted chocolate, coating the entire thing. Allow excess chocolate to drip off, then place back onto the baking sheet.

4.  Sprinkle with the topping of your choice (sprinkles, sliced almonds, etc.) while the chocolate is still wet. Slide the tray back in the refrigerator to allow the chocolate to set, about 20 minutes.

> **NOTE:** Depending on the chocolate used, these can be vegan and dairy-free.

# ENDLESS WINTER SNOWBALLS

Elsa's ill-timed cold has an undeniable upside: Not only does it introduce a remedy of Wandering Oaken's own invention, but it gives Olaf the little brothers he never knew he needed! These tiny, snowball-shaped snowmen are immortalized in Endless Winter Snowballs—a recipe inspired by Slush, Sludge, Slide, Sphere, and, of course, William. Creamy butter and almond extract are blended into a sweetened dough, then rolled into balls, coated with edible glitter, and sandwiched around a thick cream. Sweet, sparkly, and every bit as cheery as the little brothers who inspired them, Endless Winter Snowballs are immeasurably enjoyable . . . just like Olaf's adorable new relations.

**COOKIES:**

1 cup (2 sticks) unsalted butter, at room temperature
½ cup granulated sugar
1½ teaspoons vanilla extract
½ teaspoon almond extract
2 cups all-purpose flour

½ cup almond flour
¼ teaspoon salt

**FILLING:**

½ cup (1 stick) butter, softened
1½ cups confectioners' sugar

1½ teaspoons ground cinnamon
½ teaspoon almond extract
1 tablespoon heavy cream

Confectioners' sugar, for coating the cookies

1.  **TO MAKE THE COOKIES:** In a large mixing bowl with an electric mixer, cream the butter and sugar for 2 to 3 minutes until light and fluffy. Stir in the vanilla and almond extracts.

2.  In a separate large mixing bowl, whisk the all-purpose flour, almond flour, and salt. Add to the wet ingredients and mix until it forms a dough. (It will be crumbly at first.) Wrap and chill for at least 1 hour.

3.  Preheat the oven to 275°F. Line two baking sheets with parchment paper.

4.  Roll the chilled dough into 1-inch balls and place on the baking sheets. Bake for about 45 minutes, until the edges just start to turn golden. Remove and cool on the baking sheet for a few minutes, then transfer to a wire rack to cool completely.

5.  **TO MAKE THE FILLING:** In a mixing bowl, beat the butter until creamy. Gradually add the confectioners' sugar, cinnamon, and almond extract. Add the heavy cream and beat until combined.

6.  To assemble the cookies, spread some of the filling on the flat side of half the cookies, pair them with another of the same size, and press the flat sides together to create a sandwich.

7.  Place confectioners' sugar in a shallow bowl. Dip the surface of the cookies into the sugar and roll around until fully coated. (Handle with care, as the filling is soft at this point.)

8.  Chill for at least 1 hour to let the filling set, then roll the cookies in the confectioners' sugar again, if desired, to give it a more pronounced snowy effect.

# "REINDEER(S) ARE BETTER THAN PEOPLE" ANTLERS

With their lightly sweetened dough and cardamom-infused flavor, *hjortetakk*—cake doughnuts—are a well-loved Norwegian dessert. Their firm yet crisp texture, combined with their antlerlike shape, make them a popular staple at holiday parties. And their unique appearance makes them an excellent tribute to a certain singing reindeer. This recipe blends butter, eggs, and flour with the flavors of cardamom and hartshorn salt, creating a uniquely Scandinavian sweet that's sure to have everyone talking. All good things, all good things . . .

1 cup (2 sticks) unsalted butter, melted

2 cups sugar

4 eggs

1 teaspoon cardamom

1 teaspoon hartshorn (see note)

¼ cup maple syrup

½ teaspoon almond extract

4 cups all-purpose flour

Vegetable oil, for frying

**SPECIALTY TOOL:**

Kitchen thermometer

1. In a large mixing bowl, combine the melted butter and sugar. Add the eggs and beat until creamy. Stir in the cardamom, hartshorn, maple syrup, and almond extract. Gradually add the flour until a soft dough forms. Refrigerate overnight.

> **NOTE:** Hartshorn is also known as baker's ammonia or ammonium bicarbonate. Substitute 1 teaspoon baking powder and 1 teaspoon baking soda, if desired.

2. Line a plate with paper towels. In a frying pan or deep skillet, heat enough vegetable oil to submerge the cookies to 350°F. While it heats, roll the dough into 5-inch lengths and form each into rings. Use a sharp knife or kitchen scissors to make two or three nicks on the outer edge of each ring.

3. Carefully place a few pieces of shaped dough in the oil at a time. (Do not overcrowd.) Fry until golden brown, 1 to 2 minutes per side.

4. Use a slotted spoon or strainer to remove the cookies from the oil. Place on the prepared plate to drain excess oil. Cool completely.

# ROCK TROLL RICE MOUNDS

Grand Pabbie the troll has a wise word for everyone. He knows that only an act of true love can thaw a frozen heart, and that when one cannot see a future, then all they can do is the next right thing. But Arendelle's resident love expert would be stunned into silence upon tasting these chocolatey *risboller*. Rice cereal is mixed with dark chocolate, butter, and an array of sweet flavors, then mixed with berries and chopped mint. Once rolled into balls, these *risboller* are then dipped in a verdant matcha—or sprinkled with edible green glitter!—in honor of the troll family's signature moss. Cute, crunchy, and irresistibly sweet, Rock Troll Rice Mounds will be adored by everyone, from wise old trolls to fixer-uppers.

7 ounces puffed-rice cereal
½ cup dried berries (such as blueberries, blackberries, or raspberries)
Zest of 1 lemon

¼ cup fresh mint leaves, finely chopped
7 ounces dark chocolate (70% cocoa), roughly chopped
7 tablespoons unsalted butter

¾ cup confectioners' sugar
1 teaspoon vanilla extract
½ teaspoon almond extract
1 tablespoon matcha powder or green edible glitter

1. Line a baking sheet with parchment.

2. Place the puffed-rice cereal in a large mixing bowl. Add the dried berries, lemon zest, and chopped mint leaves.

3. In a medium heatproof bowl, microwave the dark chocolate and butter, in 20-second intervals, stirring each time until smooth. Stir in the confectioners' sugar and vanilla and almond extracts. Add this mixture to the cereal and stir to coat.

4. Place the matcha powder or green edible glitter in a small shallow dish.

5. Shape the cereal into small balls. Dip the top of each *risboller* into the matcha, then place on the tray. Refrigerate until set, about 1 hour.

CHAPTER SIX

# DRINKS

# SUMMER SIPPER

Ever the optimist, Olaf dreams of strolling jauntily through the summer with a cold drink in his hand. And with a bounty of berries just ripe for the picking, summertime in Scandinavia is the perfect place to do just that! This fresh Summer Sipper combines strawberries and orange juice with sparkling water and bitters for a delightfully refreshing beverage. Garnish with a festive orange peel and serve anywhere summer fun is being had—*especially* on the burning sand!

4 medium strawberries, as ripe as can be

1 ounce freshly squeezed or best-quality orange juice

3 dashes alcohol-free bitters

2 dashes alcohol-free orange bitters

1½ ounces sparkling water

Twist of orange peel, for garnish

1. Muddle 3 strawberries in the bottom of a glass, pour in the orange juice, then add the bitters and stir. Fill a tall double old-fashioned glass with ice and strain the juice into it. (This will take some patience and effort, as the muddled strawberries may clog the strainer.) Top with sparkling water. Garnish with the remaining strawberry and an orange twist.

# NONALCOHOLIC HOT GLØGG IN THE GREAT HALL

Arendelle's unexpected eternal winter sends the town into chaos. While Anna rushes off to find her sister, Hans stays behind to tend to the citizens . . . and serve hot gløgg in the castle's Great Hall. This recipe offers a nonalcoholic twist on that popular Scandinavian mulled wine by combining a variety of fruit juices with cinnamon, cloves, and the classic Norse flavor, cardamom. With hints of orange and star anise, Nonalcoholic Hot Gløgg in the Great Hall will warm any heart—villainous, frozen, or otherwise!

96 fluid ounces mix of fruit juices (cranberry, cherry, pomegranate, and apple, no sugar added)

½ cup raisins

8 dried figs, quartered

3 cinnamon sticks, plus more for garnish

10 green cardamom pods

2 star anise pods

Two 2-inch strips orange peel

¼ cup sugar, plus more as needed

1 tablespoon whole cloves

¼ cup blanched almonds

Orange slices, for garnish (optional)

1. In a large pot, heat the fruit juices with the raisins, figs, cinnamon sticks, cardamom pods, star anise pods, strips of orange peel, sugar, and cloves over medium-high heat. Bring to nearly a boil, then lower the heat to low, cover, and simmer for 30 minutes. Add the almonds.

2. Ladle the gløgg into clear mugs. Spoon some of each of the raisins, figs, and almonds into each mug, taking care to remove and discard any cardamom pods, star anise, or cloves. Garnish with a cinnamon stick and a slice of orange, if you'd like.

3. Sweeten to taste with additional sugar, if you wish.

# HOT TUB HOT CHOCOLATE

Olaf knows the value of downtime. The lively snowman takes a break from his quest to discover *all* the holiday traditions to examine a Norway-shaped cookie, taste a fruitcake, and dance with kittens. But it's when he imagines summer—and soaking in a tub with a steamy cup of cocoa—that he hits peak levels of relaxation. Hot Tub Hot Chocolate takes Olaf's imagined happy place to a whole new level. With creamy milk and rich dark chocolate, this wonderfully warm beverage can be shared by children, adults, and snow-people alike. After all, some people are worth melting for . . . just maybe not right this second.

**RYE SIMPLE SYRUP:**

1 cup water

1 cup sugar

¼ cup rye flour

**HOT CHOCOLATE:**

2 cups whole milk

2 ounces dark chocolate, chopped

2 tablespoons Dutch-process cocoa powder, plus more for dusting

¼ cup rye simple syrup

Marshmallows, for serving

Pinch smoked salt, for serving

1. **TO MAKE THE RYE SIMPLE SYRUP:** In a medium saucepan over medium-high heat, combine the water and sugar and bring to a boil, stirring constantly until the sugar is dissolved. Add the rye flour and stir over low heat until it thickens slightly, about 4 minutes. Remove from the heat and allow to cool. Strain through a fine-mesh sieve into a jar.

2. **TO MAKE THE HOT CHOCOLATE:** Heat the milk in a saucepan over medium-low heat, stirring occasionally, until it's steaming. Remove it from the heat and stir in the chopped chocolate, stirring until melted and smooth. Whisk in the cocoa powder and salt until smooth and there are no lumps.

3. Stir in the simple syrup, adjusting the quantity to your desired sweetness.

4. Pour into two mugs, float marshmallows in the hot chocolate, sprinkle with smoked salt, and enjoy.

**NOTE:** This recipe is easy to make dairy-free with dairy-free milk and dairy-free chocolates and cocoa powder.

# NORDIC TEA SERVICE

The sweater-loving Wandering Oaken is an Arendellian of many talents. In addition to running his trading post (and sauna!), he peddles sunscreen and cold remedies of his own invention and operates a seasonal outdoor spa—complete with nail treatments and a relaxing tea. Nordic Tea Service offers a serene twist on Oaken's outdoor offering, pairing black tea with dried lavender and rose petals and adding the uniquely Scandinavian flavors of elderflower and juniper. Steeped into a hot tea and best served in the open air, Nordic Tea Service is a refreshing custom that makes for a rejuvenating follow-up to any big summer blowout.

½ cup Assam black tea leaves

½ cup Ceylon black tea leaves

½ cup dried culinary-grade rose petals

¼ cup dried culinary-grade lavender flowers

⅓ cup dried elderberries

⅓ cup dried juniper berries

¼ cup dried licorice root

¼ cup chopped dried orange peel

**SPECIALTY TOOLS:**

Spice grinder or mortar and pestle

1. Place the Assam and Ceylon teas, rose petals, and lavender in a jar.

2. In a spice grinder, pulse the elderberries and juniper berries to break them up. Add to the jar. Top with the licorice root and orange peel. Cover and shake to combine.

3. To serve, add tea to a tea strainer or compostable tea bag in a cup or pot. (Use 1 heaping tablespoon tea per 1 cup boiling water.) Pour water over the tea and steep for 4 to 5 minutes.

4. Enjoy the tea black, or add cream and sweeten with the vanilla-, licorice-, and lavender-infused simple syrup from the "Let It G(l)o(w)" Snowy Cream Soda (page 123).

5. Store unused dried tea blend in an airtight container for up to several months.

**VARIATION:** If you like a little smoke, a pinch of *lapsang souchong* would be beautiful here.

**NOTE:** If you don't have a spice grinder, a mortar and pestle will do.

# "LET IT G(L)O(W)" SNOWY CREAM SODA

Elsa's special brand of magic has delightfully dazzling outcomes: She's able to channel icy chandeliers, form frosty bridges, and summon snowy sculptures. This sparkling soda brings together the best of Elsa's powers, evoking the creamy color of snow and the glittery glow of magic. With a dollop of dried lavender and a dose of licorice, "Let It G(l)o(w)" Snowy Cream Soda is a blizzard-worthy blend that's best served chilled . . . so long as one's not bothered by the cold, anyway.

1 vanilla bean

1 cup water

¾ cup sugar

1 tablespoon culinary-grade dried lavender

2 teaspoons dried licorice root

2 cups cold sparkling water or club soda

1 teaspoon edible luster dust

Ice, for serving

2 tablespoons heavy cream or half-and-half

1. Use the tip of a sharp knife to split the vanilla bean in half lengthwise. Scrape out the seeds using the back of the knife.

2. In a medium saucepan over medium heat, combine the water, sugar, dried lavender, licorice root, and vanilla bean and seeds until the sugar dissolves, about 5 minutes. Remove from the heat and allow the lavender and licorice to steep while the syrup cools. After about 30 minutes, strain through a fine-mesh sieve into a jar to remove the solids. Refrigerate until cold.

3. To make the cream sodas, add 3 tablespoons syrup to each of two glasses. Divide the club soda and edible luster dust between them and stir to combine. Add ice to fill the glasses, then top with 1 tablespoon cream over each, or more to taste.

4. Store the remaining simple syrup in the refrigerator, covered in an airtight container, for up to 2 weeks.

# FROZEN FRACTALS FRUIT JUICE

When a lyrical voice summons Elsa into the unknown, she initially resists the call. After all, everyone she loves is right there with her in Arendelle . . . and no good could possibly come from following a secret siren on an entirely unpredictable adventure. Frozen Fractals Fruit Juice reimagines the mysterious voice as an enchanting, whimsical libation. Sweet, light, and brimming with magic, this juice summons the spirit of *saft*—a popular fruit-based Scandinavian beverage. It's perfect for toasting with friends before embarking on a shared adventure—unknown or otherwise. *Skål!*

4 cups water

1 cup sugar

12 dried butterfly pea flowers

2 sprigs thyme, plus more for serving

Ice, for serving

1 cup freshly squeezed lemon juice (from about 6 large lemons)

1. In a small saucepan over medium-high heat, heat the water, sugar, butterfly pea flowers, and thyme, stirring occasionally, until the sugar dissolves. Allow to cool, then strain into a jar and discard the solids.

2. To serve, fill four glasses with ice. Divide the butterfly pea flower syrup between the glasses. Pour in the lemon juice and garnish with additional thyme sprigs.

# APPLE CIDER "WORTH MELTING FOR"

Olaf knows that some people are worth melting for. The loyal snowman risks his own life to help the freezing Anna, building a fire—and learning what warmth feels like!—to ensure she holds on. This spicy apple cider invokes the flavors of the North to create a beverage that could warm even the coldest heart. With apples, lingonberry, cinnamon, and cardamom, Apple Cider "Worth Melting For" will bring to mind Olaf's wise words: "So this is heat. I love it!"

4 cups apple juice or apple cider

¼ cup lingonberry preserves

2 cinnamon sticks, plus more for serving

4 cardamom pods

1 large strip of orange peel

4 whole cloves

4 whole allspice berries

1 star anise pod, plus more for serving

Sugar or honey, for serving (optional)

2 tablespoons dried unsweetened cranberries

1. In a medium saucepan over medium heat, combine the apple juice or cider, lingonberry preserves, cinnamon sticks, cardamom pods, orange peel, cloves, allspice berries, and star anise pod. Bring to a gentle simmer, then lower to low heat and simmer for about 15 minutes, adjusting the heat as needed. Strain out the spices and solids, reserving the liquid in a jar.

2. Taste and add a little sugar or honey if you want a sweeter cider.

3. Divide among four mugs, add dried cranberries to each, and garnish with additional cinnamon sticks or star anise, if desired.

# CONCLUSION

From the frosty fjords to the icy North Mountain, the wintry world of Frozen invokes images of snow-dusted trails and trees dripping with icicles. Olaf's magical forest shows Anna how beautiful winter can be, whereas Marshmallow's roaring rage sends the princess, the ice harvester, the reindeer, and the snowman on a powdery plunge. The warm and savory recipes charmingly captured within these pages summon the spirited nature of our Frozen friends' cold-weather follies—from Are Reindeers Better Than People? Glazed Carrots (page 35) to Trading Post Ham and Potato Dumplings (page 63). And the summery season of Scandinavia's never-ending midnight sun is honored by dishes so light and crisp, they're sure to summon a sense of fantastical fun. Cool as a Cucumber Salad with Dill (page 25) calls upon Olaf's summery imaginings, whereas Fruits of the Enchanted Forest Sorbet (page 92) invokes the flavors of the Enchanted Forest. And beloved classics—from "What's That Amazing Smell?" Chocolate Torte (page 103) to Ice Miners Sugar Cookies (page 106)—are on hand year-round to fuel adventurous sessions of snowplay . . . or building castles atop the burning sand!

We hope you've enjoyed your journey through Anna and Elsa's magical world. With more than 60 recipes to choose from—each made from a slew of seasonal ingredients just ripe for the picking (or foraging!)—the magic within these pages will keep you cooking through long winter nights and sun-filled summer days. From the time-honored treat Rustic Winter Rice Porridge (page 15) to the universally adored "Acts of True Love" Norwegian Heart Waffles (page 21), this Scandinavian tome of culinary classics will ensure that anyone who loves Frozen never has to "Let It Go." *Takk for maten!*

# GLOSSARY

**BEAT:** To blend ingredients and/or incorporate air into a mixture by vigorously whisking, stirring, or using a handheld or stand mixer.

**BLENDER:** Blends or purées sauces and soups to varying textures, from chunky to perfectly smooth. Also used to make smoothies and shakes.

**BUTTER:** Unless otherwise noted, recipes call for salted butter.

**BUTTERFLY PEA FLOWERS:** These dried flower blossoms are commonly used in herbal tea drinks. When added to a recipe, they provide a beautiful deep blue color. If combined with acids, like lemon juice, the color turns to pink or purple. They are available online and in some health food stores. They are also turned into a powder and an extract.

**CANDY THERMOMETER:** Sometimes called a fry thermometer, this long glass instrument can be clipped to the side of a pot. It can withstand temperature of at least 500°F and is used to measure the temperature of frying oil or sugar when making syrups, candies, and certain frostings.

**CARDAMOM, FRESHLY GROUND:** Cardamom is frequently used in Scandinavian baking. For best results, buy cardamom pods or seeds rather than ground cardamom, and grind the cardamom seeds each time you need them, using a spice grinder.

**COLANDER:** Separates liquids from solids by draining the liquid through the small holes in the bowl.

**CONFECTIONERS' SUGAR:** Also called powdered sugar, this is granulated sugar that has been ground into a powdered state. It's primarily used to make smooth icings and for dusting finished baked goods.

**DRY MEASURING CUPS:** Measuring tools that usually come in sizes of ¼ cup, ⅓ cup, ½ cup, and 1 cup. They are ideal for measuring dry ingredients such as flour, sugar, rice, and pasta.

**DUTCH OVEN:** A large (usually 5- to 6-quart), heavy cooking pot ideal for making stews, braises, and deep-fried foods. Dutch ovens are often made from cast iron or enameled cast iron, which makes them hold and distribute heat evenly. A Dutch oven works well when cooking at either high or low temperatures, making it a versatile vessel and handy addition to every kitchen.

**EGG WASH:** A mixture used to create a sheen or gloss on breads, pastries, and other baked goods. Whisk together one egg and 1 tablespoon water until light and foamy. Use a pastry brush to apply before baking when the recipe requires.

**EMULSIFY:** This refers to the process of combining two ingredients that do not typically mix easily, such as oil and vinegar.

**FOLDING IN:** This refers to gently adding an ingredient with a spatula in wide, gentle strokes. Do not whisk or stir vigorously. Folding allows any airiness already established to stay intact.

**FOOD PROCESSOR:** A motorized machine with a bowl and a variety of removable blades used for chopping, shredding, slicing, and blending ingredients. A food processor can be used to prepare vegetables, fruits, and cheeses for cooking as well as to blend sauces and dips.

**FRYING PAN:** A shallow, round cooking vessel used primarily for stovetop cooking. It's good to have a range of sizes. Generally, a small frying pan or skillet is 6 inches across, a medium skillet is 8 inches across, a large skillet is 10 inches across, and an extra-large skillet is 12 inches across.

**GEITOST (AKA GJETOST AND BRUNOST):** A Norwegian brown cheese that's creamy and slightly sweet, made with either goat milk or a mix of cow and goat milk.

**GRANULATED SUGAR:** A highly refined sugar made from sugar cane or sugar beets, known for its white color and fine texture. All the molasses has been removed from this type of sugar.

**GREASING A PAN:** Coating a pan with nonstick cooking spray, oil, softened butter, or shortening to keep (usually) baked goods such as cakes from sticking.

**HIGH-HEAT vs. NONSTICK PANS:** A high-heat pan—as its name suggests—can stand up to high-heat cooking, generally temperatures between 400°F and 600°F. It's usually made of stainless steel, cast iron, or enameled cast iron and can be used on the stovetop or oven—if the handle is made of an ovenproof material. Nonstick cookware contains a coating that helps keeps foods from sticking (particularly eggs), but it can't be used at the same temperatures as a high-heat pan. If you are cooking with nonstick cookware, make sure you know the manufacturer's heat limits for it. Most nonstick cookware should not be used at above medium heat on a stovetop (about 350°F) and is not generally suitable for the oven.

**LAPSANG SOUCHONG:** A black tea with distinctly smoky aroma and flavor.

**LIQUID MEASURING CUPS:** Clear glass or plastic tools used for measuring precise amounts of liquids by lining up the level of liquid to the marks on the cup. Useful sizes include 1 cup, 2 cups, and 4 cups.

**MEASURING SPOONS:** A set of measuring tools used to accurately portion smaller amounts of ingredients. They usually come in a set that includes ⅛ teaspoon, ¼ teaspoon, ½ teaspoon, 1 teaspoon, and 1 tablespoon. They can be used for liquid ingredients such as vinegar, juices, oils, and extracts and dry ingredients such as flour, salt, sugar, and spices.

**MILK:** Unless otherwise noted, these recipes call for dairy milk. In most cases, any percentage of milk fat will do.

**MUDDLE:** A short-handled tool that is textured on one end and used to mash together ingredients such as fruits, herbs, and sugar when making flavored drinks.

**PARCHMENT PAPER:** Food-safe paper that can withstand temperatures of up to 450°F—even up to 500°F for short baking times—that's used to line pans for baking and roasting. Parchment paper keeps foods from sticking and makes cleanup easier.

**PIPING FROSTING:** The process of decorating cakes and cookies by squeezing frosting placed in a decorating bag over them. Piping can be done with or without a decorating tip—or even in a plastic bag with one corner snipped off to allow the frosting to be applied in a neat rope shape.

**ROLLING PIN:** A long, cylindrical tool—most often made of wood—used to flatten and roll out dough when making breads and pastries.

**RUBBER SPATULA:** A handled tool with a flat, flexible blade used to fold ingredients together and to scrape the sides of bowls clean.

**SALT:** Unless otherwise noted, use your salt of choice in the recipes in this book. Kosher salt—which is coarser than regular table salt—is generally recommended for the recipes throughout this book.

**SAUCEPAN WITH LID:** A round, deep cooking vessel used for boiling or simmering. It is useful to have a range of sizes, including 1 quart, 2 quarts, 3 quarts, and 4 quarts.

**SEAR:** To create a crust on a piece of meat, poultry, or fish by placing it in a very hot pan or on a very hot grill. The high heat quickly caramelizes the natural sugars in the food, creating a deeply browned and flavorful crust. Once the crust is formed, the heat is usually turned down so that the interior of the meat can cook properly without burning the outside.

**SIFT:** The process of putting flour, confectioners' sugar, or cornstarch through a fine-mesh sieve to aerate and remove lumps. Multiple ingredients—such as flour, salt, and leavenings—are often sifted together to blend them.

**SILICONE BAKING MAT:** Used to line shallow baking pans when making foods such as cookies and pastries to prevent sticking. They can withstand high temperatures in the oven and can also be used in the freezer. Dough can be rolled out on them, and they can easily go from prep station to chilling to the oven without having to move the dough. They are easy to clean and reusable.

**SIMMER:** To cook a liquid such as a sauce or soup at low-enough heat so that bubbles are just barely breaking over the surface.

**SPATULA/PANCAKE TURNER:** A handled tool with a wide, flexible blade used to flip or turn foods during cooking.

**SPICE GRINDER:** Available in electric and manual forms. This book calls for freshly ground cardamom in many recipes; consider keeping an inexpensive manual spice grinder filled with a few tablespoons of cardamom seeds for this purpose.

**STAND MIXER:** A heavy-duty machine with a large bowl and various attachments used to mix, beat, or whip foods at varying speeds. Stand mixers are advised for making heavy, dense, or stiff doughs for cookies or yeasted breads.

**VANILLA PASTE vs. VANILLA EXTRACT:** Vanilla bean paste provides strong vanilla flavor and beautiful vanilla bean flecks without having to split and scrape a vanilla bean. Although it is more expensive than extract, there are situations in which it really elevates the finished dish. When that's the case, a recipe will specifically call for vanilla bean paste, but it can always be replaced in a 1-to-1 ratio with vanilla extract.

**WHIP:** To use a whisk or electric mixer to aerate ingredients such as egg whites and heavy cream to lighten, stiffen, and form peaks.

**WHISK:** A handled tool with thin wires arranged in various shapes used for mixing and whipping liquids and batters to combine ingredients or incorporate air into them. The two most common types of whisks are the balloon whisk, which has a bulbous end that narrows down toward the handle, and the sauce whisk, which has a round coil that sits flat on the bottom of the pan.

# CONVERSION CHARTS

KITCHEN MEASUREMENTS

| CUPS | TABLESPOONS | TEASPOONS | FLUID OUNCES |
|------|-------------|-----------|--------------|
| ¹⁄₁₆ cup | 1 tbsp | 3 tsp | ½ fl oz |
| ⅛ cup | 2 tbsp | 6 tsp | 1 fl oz |
| ¼ cup | 4 tbsp | 12 tsp | 2 fl oz |
| ⅓ cup | 5½ tbsp | 16 tsp | 2⅔ fl oz |
| ½ cup | 8 tbsp | 24 tsp | 4 fl oz |
| ⅔ cup | 10⅔ tbsp | 32 tsp | 5⅓ fl oz |
| ¾ cup | 12 tbsp | 36 tsp | 6 fl oz |
| 1 cup | 16 tbsp | 48 tsp | 8 fl oz |

| GALLONS | QUARTS | PINTS | CUPS | FLUID OUNCES |
|---------|--------|-------|------|--------------|
| ¹⁄₁₆ gal | ¼ qt | ½ pt | 1 cup | 8 fl oz |
| ⅛ gal | ½ qt | 1 pt | 2 cups | 16 fl oz |
| ¼ gal | 1 qt | 2 pt | 4 cups | 32 fl oz |
| ½ gal | 2 qt | 4 pt | 8 cups | 64 fl oz |
| 1 gal | 4 qt | 8 pt | 16 cups | 128 fl oz |

## WEIGHT

| GRAMS | OUNCES |
|-------|--------|
| 14 g  | ½ oz   |
| 28 g  | 1 oz   |
| 57 g  | 2 oz   |
| 85 g  | 3 oz   |
| 113 g | 4 oz   |
| 142 g | 5 oz   |
| 170 g | 6 oz   |
| 283 g | 10 oz  |
| 397 g | 14 oz  |
| 454 g | 16 oz  |
| 907 g | 32 oz  |

## OVEN TEMPERATURES

| FAHRENHEIT | CELSIUS |
|------------|---------|
| 200°F      | 93°C    |
| 225°F      | 107°C   |
| 250°F      | 121°C   |
| 275°F      | 135°C   |
| 300°F      | 149°C   |
| 325°F      | 163°C   |
| 350°F      | 177°C   |
| 375°F      | 191°C   |
| 400°F      | 204°C   |
| 425°F      | 218°C   |
| 450°F      | 232°C   |

## LENGTH

| IMPERIAL | METRIC  |
|----------|---------|
| 1 in     | 2.5 cm  |
| 2 in     | 5 cm    |
| 4 in     | 10 cm   |
| 6 in     | 15 cm   |
| 8 in     | 20 cm   |
| 10 in    | 25 cm   |
| 12 in    | 30 cm   |

# DIETARY CONSIDERATIONS

V: Vegetarian | V*: Easily made vegetarian | V+: Vegan | V+*: Easily made vegan
GF: Gluten-free | GF*: Easily made gluten-free | DF: Dairy-free | DF*: Easily made dairy-free

## CHAPTER ONE:
## BREAKFAST

Castle Mornings Granola with Rhubarb Compote: **V, GF*, DF***

Picnic Raisin Buns: **V**

Rustic Winter Rice Porridge: **V, GF**

Eggerøre with Parsley, Chives, and Pea Vines: **V, GF**

"Two Sisters, One Mind" Pancakes: **V**

"Act of True Love" Norwegian Heart Waffles: **V**

## CHAPTER TWO:
## APPETIZERS, SIDES, AND SALADS

Fish Throwers Gravlax with Sweet Mustard Sauce: **GF, DF**

Cool as a Cucumber Salad with Dill: **V, V+, GF, DF**

Coronation Day Shrimp Canapés: **GF***

Fire-Roasted Breadsticks: **V**

8,000 Salad Plates Salad: **V, V+, GF, DF**

Forever Winter Barley Salad: **V**

Are Reindeers Better Than People? Glazed Carrots with Orange and Parsley: **V, GF, DF**

"Certain Certainties" Butter-Braised Red Potatoes: **V, GF**

Palace Steps Royal Potatoes: **V**

## CHAPTER THREE:
## SOUPS

Town Square Spinach Soup: **V, GF***

Pumpkin Patch Beef Stew: **GF**

Frozen Fjord Fish Soup: **GF**

"Hot Soup and Gløgg in the Great Hall" Yellow Pea Soup: **GF**

## CHAPTER FOUR:
## ENTRÉES

"Within These Walls" Pytt i Panne: **GF**

"Every Autumn Breeze" Fårikål

### FISH

Fire-Roasted Salmon with Creamy Herb Sauce: **GF**

Not-Quite Lutefisk: Pan-Seared Cod with Cream Sauce and Blackberries: **GF**

Scandinavian Fish Cakes with Mustard Cream Sauce

Foreign Lands Bacalao: **GF**

### CHICKEN

Cozy Fricassee of Chicken

"Soup, Roast, and Ice Cream" Roast Chicken with Brown Gravy and Herb Sauce

"We Finish Each Other's Sandwiches" Chicken Salad on Rye Bread

### PORK

Trading Post Ham and Potato Dumplings: **DF**

Burning Love: **GF**

"Lost in the Woods" Juniper-Scented Pork Chops with Morels and Peas

Roasted Pork with Cherry Sauce: **GF**

### BEEF

A Thousand Reasons Meatballs

Steak with Creamy Wild Mushrooms

Coronation Day Herb-Crusted Prime Rib with Blueberry Au Jus and Horseradish Sauce

Sailors Beef Stew

## CHAPTER FIVE:
## DESSERTS

Brown Butter Lefse with Spiced Pears and Thyme: **V**

Homemade "Do You Want to Build a Snowman?" Ice Cream: **V, GF**

Personal Flurry Pavlova: **V, GF***

Troll Cream: **V, GF**

Snow Cone Ice Monster: **V, GF, DF**

Northern Lights Ice Pops: **V, GF***

Fruits of the Enchanted Forest Sorbet: **V, V+, GF, DF**

"Split the Ice Apart" Panna Cotta: **GF**

## CAKES

Ice Palace Kransekake:
**V, GF\*, DF**

Coronation Day Princess Cake

Fixer-Upper Carrot Cake: **V**

Thaw the Winter Cake: **V**

"What's That Amazing
Smell?" Chocolate Torte: **V**

## COOKIES

Frozen Fractals Gingersnaps: **V**

Ice Miners Sugar Cookies: **V**

"Shove Some Chocolate
in My Face" Marzipan
Truffles: **V, V+\*, GF, DF**

Endless Winter Snowballs: **V**

"Reindeer(s) Are Better
Than People" Antlers: **V**

Rock Troll Rice Mounds: **V**

## CHAPTER SIX:
# DRINKS

Summer Sipper: **V, V+, GF, DF**

Nonalcoholic Hot Gløgg in
the Great Hall: **V, V+, GF, DF**

Hot Tub Hot Chocolate: **V**

Nordic Tea Service:
**V, V+, GF, DF**

"Let It G(l)o(w)" Snowy
Cream Soda: **V, GF**

Frozen Fractals Fruit
Juice: **V, V+, GF, DF**

Apple Cider "Worth Melting
For": **V, V+, GF, DF**

# FRY STATION SAFETY TIPS

If you're making something that requires deep-frying, here are some important tips to prevent any kitchen fires:

- If you don't have a dedicated deep fryer, use a Dutch oven or a high-walled sauté pan.

- Never have too much oil in the pan! You don't want hot oil spilling out as soon as you put the food in.

- Only use a suitable cooking oil, like canola, peanut, or vegetable oil.

- Always keep track of the oil temperature with a thermometer—350°F to 375°F should do the trick.

- Never put too much food in the pan at the same time!

- Never put wet food in the pan. It will splatter and may cause burns.

- Always have a lid nearby to cover the pan in case it starts to spill over or catch fire. A properly rated fire extinguisher is also great to have on hand in case of emergencies.

- Never leave the pan unattended, and never let children near the pan.

- Never, ever put your face, hand, or any other body part in the hot oil.

# ABOUT THE
# AUTHORS

**DAYTONA DANIELSEN** is a novelist and cookbook author whose fiction and food writing evokes the forests, fjords, and folklore of her Norwegian heritage. She holds an MFA in fiction from Pacific University and lives near Seattle, Washington, with her two children. Find more at her website, Daytonadanielsen.com.

**S. T. BENDE** is a young-adult and children's author, known for the Norse mythology series Viking Academy and the Ære Saga. She's also written books for Disney, Lucasfilm, Pixar, the Jim Henson Company and Marvel. She lives on the West Coast, where she spends far too much time at Disneyland, and she dreams of skiing on Jotunheim and Hoth. You can find her at www.stbende.com.

# AUTHOR ACKNOWLEGMENTS

➤————————€

The creation of this book took place while I was in grad school, writing a novel, and working to support myself and my children as a single mom. Somehow, this time didn't feel harried, but rather was rich and life-giving thanks to everyone who gave me grace and space to do the work and who encouraged me along the way.

First, Vincent and Audrey Strong, I love being your mom. It was a joy creating this book in this season of our lives together, and I appreciate your patience, inspiration, and enthusiasm. Vincent, I loved watching your ideas for the Snow Cone Ice Monster and Endless Winter Snowballs come to life. Audrey, your enthusiasm while creating your Thaw the Winter Cake and Ice Miners Sugar Cookies was a delight.

Dad and Mom (Roar and Sandi Danielsen), you help me remember that any dream is possible. These pages are full of memories and moments that you helped me to realize, whether through travel, baking, or doing the dishes! Similarly, the influence of my grandparents—Lowell and Adeline Midstokke, and Lauritz and Agny Danielsen—is woven through these pages, as they showed me our Norwegian heritage through countless meals and cookies while I was growing up.

Thank you, Sean Patrick Coon, for your endless love, and Sarah Madson for your enduring belief. And to my fantastic editor Anna Wostenberg, coauthor S. T. Bende, and Elsa, Anna, Sven, Olaf, and everyone else who had a hand in creating this book—I'm proud to have created this with you.

**DAYTONA DANIELSEN**


To my boys, who always say yes to Norwegian waffles, and never laugh too hard when I run through Disneyland to meet Elsa. (And she calls me out for it.) *Jeg elsker deg!* And to Olaug, for sharing her recipes and making us her family—*takk for maten!*

Thanks to D23 for those first early glimpses of *Let It Go* and *Some Things Never Change*. (*Jeg beklager* again to the kiddo I may have launched off my lap during my enthusiastic standing ovation!) Warm hugs to my Norse crew. *Tusen takk* to the magical team at Disney for a lifetime of inspiration, and to the Imagineers who brought Arendelle to life in the parks. And of course, a very hearty *skål* to Samantha. Wait—I don't even know a Samantha . . .

**S. T. BENDE**

# INDEX

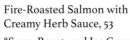

INSIGHT
EDITIONS

PO Box 3088
San Rafael, CA 94912
www.insighteditions.com

ISBN: 979-8-88663-543-0

Publisher: Raoul Goff
SVP, Group Publisher: Vanessa Lopez
VP, Creative: Chrissy Kwasnik
VP, Manufacturing: Alix Nicholaeff
Art Director: Stuart Smith
Designer: Brooke McCullum
Senior Editor: Anna Wostenberg
Editorial Assistant: Sami Alvarado
VP, Senior Executive Project Editor: Vicki Jaeger
Production Manager: Deena Hashem
Senior Production Manager, Subsidiary Rights: Lina s Palma-Temena

Photographer: Ted Thomas
Food and Prop Stylist: Elena Craig
Assistant Food Stylists: Lauren Tedeschi and Patricia Parrish

 ROOTS of PEACE  REPLANTED PAPER

Insight Editions, in association with Roots of Peace, will plant two trees for each tree used in the manufacturing of this book. Roots of Peace is an internationally renowned humanitarian organization dedicated to eradicating land mines worldwide and converting war-torn lands into productive farms and wildlife habitats. Roots of Peace will plant two million fruit and nut trees in Afghanistan and provide farmers there with the skills and support necessary for sustainable land use.

Manufactured in China by Insight Editions

10 9 8 7 6 5 4 3 2 1